CAMPFIRE TALES
and other adventures

CAMPFIRE
Tales
and other adventures

RON MCCOY

Published by *Many* SEASONS
2018 | Mesa, Arizona

Campfire Tales and other adventures
Ron McCoy © 2018
Cover and book design by Yolie Hernandez, AZBookDesigner@icloud.com
Cover picture: iStock: 840935324 Diane39

Published by *Many* SEASONS
123 N. Centennial Way, Suite 237
Mesa, AZ 85201
480-939-9689

First Edition
Campfire Tales and other adventures
1st. ed. pp. x. 126
ISBN-978-1-936885-27-5
Printed in the United States of America.
1 2 3 4 5 6 7 8 9 10

No part of this book may be used, saved, scanned, or reproduced in any manner whatsoever without the written permission of the author and/or publisher.

All Rights Reserved.

CONTENTS

Acknowledgements vii
Introduction ix
Lefty and the X Trail 1
Betty and my Squeaky Saddle 5
Trail Ride in Parker, Colorado 7
Ron and the Umbrella 9
Lost In Tranquility 11
The Who, When and Where 13
When Do You Become Too Old To Ride? 15
The Breaking of Lefty 17
Rattlesnake Canyon 21
John Selling Horse 25
John's Black Bear 27
The Saddle Rock Ranch 31
Dumped In Cactus 33
The Second Long Horn Roundup 35
TAASOSPSB 39

Uninvited Dinner Guest 43

Picking Up Trash Has Some Hazards 45

Roundup Interruption 47

Suitcase Surprise 49

What *Wuz* That? 51

How Much Will A Horse Cost Me? 53

The Wreck 55

Alamo Canyon Passage Trail 57

Accident on the Trail 61

Never Look a Gift Horse in The Mouth 65

A Really Great Experience 69

There Is a Real Ol' Wild Bill 71

I Know How They Must Have Felt 79

I Know You've Seen These Folks on the Trail 81

Good Judgement in Trailer Loading 83

The Arizona Stage Line 87

Sheplers Western Wear 89

Demise of a Good Hat and a Pair of Boots 91

103 Degrees in Goldfield 93

Don't Know Where the Trails Are 97

Journal Entries 99

Arizona Guest Ranch Ride 107

Another Round Up In Holbrook 109

Shelly and the Snake 115

The Time I Broke Something 117

Closing Statement 119

Recipes for Hungry Folks on the Trail 121

ACKNOWLEDGEMENTS

CAN'T THANK THOSE OF YOU OUT THERE ENOUGH for your support, help and sharing of wisdom.

Many thanks to the Apache Junction Writer's Club, in particularly to: LB Winn, President; John Nudge and Cathie Reinterring.

I appreciate the input from my four daughters over the years: Debbie Gregory, Katy DiGiovanni, Thea Ammons and Sara Davis.

Many thanks to the Directors and Members of the Indiana Trail Riders Association, especially to: Greg Hersberger, Jody Weldy, Arlene Smoot and Larry Sidell. You have provided the inspiration for many of my stories.

A big thanks to "Big" Mike McDaniels and Roz Rosbrook, both of whom influenced my ambitions early on.

Special tribute to old "Wild" Bill Stites, my best friend for over the last 60 years or so, who has had adventures we could all be envious of.

Many authors find their heartfelt appreciation goes to their spouse and mine goes to my wife, Karen, for typing, correcting, editing and pushing me forward. Thanks honey, I love you.

INTRODUCTION

I KNOW MOST FOLKS DON'T READ BOOK INTRODUCTIONS, prefaces, or the like. Certainly I never do. However, I'm putting a few words down to introduce my book, a collection of short stories. Some are very short. And a few are tips I've collected over some 60 years of owning and riding horses. All are based on events that actually happened. I've omitted or changed a few of the names in places to avoid embarrassing or offending someone.

Life and our current society have put a lot of pressure on people not to go about life at a leisurely pace. It is almost un-American to go about leisurely. The interstate demands that we drive at a high rate of speed from one McDonald's, Burger King, Budget Inn, Holiday Inn, Flying J, Texaco and Shell gas stations to the next one, paying little heed to the scenery or life between them. The electronic age of e-mail, text messaging, and so on, eliminates the personal one-on-one contact we used to have, which we referred to it at that time as having a conversation. The other day at a mall, I saw two young girls, perhaps 12 or so, sitting on a bench rapidly and energetically texting. After a moment or two, I realized they were texting each other. What's that all about? A friend of mine observed at a nice restaurant several adults and some teenage children all of who sat in silence while they were texting. What are we coming to? I frequently ask folks what they did the night before and I always get the expected response, "watched TV." My reply is usually, "What did you watch?"

Now with a confused look I get the usual answer, "I don't know. I don't remember."

I have seen many people sitting by a campfire or watching a babbling brook, maybe sitting on a beach watching the waves coming in, or perhaps riding a horse on a fall day crunching through the newly fallen leaves. Or even experiencing a slow falling rain or watching snow collect on the windows while sitting by a warm fire, perhaps with light conversation with someone they care about and then remember years later the whole scene as if it were yesterday.

My hope, desire and wish is that these stories will refresh your memory of something from the past or give you the desire to do something in the future at a leisurely pace, and taking the proverbial time to stop and smell the roses.

LEFTY AND THE X TRAIL

THE SPRING IN 2000, brought a new six-mile trail to Versailles State Park in Indiana. I'd been told that it would be open for sure in the spring. So on the Friday before Memorial Day, figuring it would be open by then, Karen and I decided to check it out.

We used to live about 40 minutes from Versailles State Park, the second largest State Park in Indiana, which has about 5,900 acres. Upon our arrival there, we quickly saddled up and rode out and by golly there was no new X Trail in sight. I was disappointed to say the least, but we did have a nice ride of seven and a half miles on A Loop. We were almost back to the day use area when Karen suddenly pulled up her horse and pointing to a sign that said "X Trail," commented that she hadn't noticed that sign there on the way out. Neither one of us could believe that we would have missed it.

We decided to follow the sign and as we rode, more trail markers began to appear along the trail. Pretty soon we came up to a park employee in his truck, busily unloading more signs for X Trail. They had just opened it! Our time running short, we were unable to stay on the trail any longer that day. That would be another adventure for another day.

Eager to try the new X Trail, I decided to try it out the following week. Karen was at work that day and Sara was in school, so I had nothing else better to do. It didn't take long to gather up my gear and load up my "goes anywhere, does anything horse." The park is fairly quiet on the weekdays, and is a day-use only facility. On the weekends, it's a different story; full house.

I ride with my spurs on whenever I ride my horse, Lefty, as he can get kind of lazy. I've got a pair of really old boots full of holes, with worn out heels and soles that I keep my spurs on and just leave them on. Whenever I ride, I change into those boots before jumping into the saddle.

The first part of X Trail is wide and is in excellent condition. It winds around and comes to a creek that runs through a tunnel that goes under Highway 50 to another part of the park. On the other side there were several very pretty small waterfalls over which the trail goes, and it continues through the creek a little way further until you hit a regular trail again. Now, in reality, this is not as intimidating as it might sound to those who haven't seen it. Since I was on Lefty, "my goes anywhere, does anything horse," he plodded along quite nicely taking it all in.

Altogether X Trail is about six miles with a Y loop of two miles, and more recently a Z loop of probably another two miles. There were four or five places that were really muddy, but have since been fixed. We got through the bad places okay and had a super ride. Before long we headed back and had made our way back to the creek where the pretty little waterfalls were. On the last one it was a step down of about 12 inches with water running over it from sheer side bank to sheer side bank. It was there that my "goes anywhere, does anything horse" absolutely refused to step down. I tried unsuccessfully for ten minutes to get Lefty to take that step. No luck. I knew I'd have to get off and lead him. This usually worked, except this time. There I was wading around in several inches of water. Remember those old boots I was wearing?

I tried to push him off. That didn't work. I got behind him and shoved him with a "come on old fat horse." He wouldn't budge. Last resort measures were in order. I stepped off the ledge into the drink, water to my knees. I stretched the reins out in front of him. Now as most of you know, in this situation a horse will jump straight towards you. So with my great wisdom and experience kicking in, I took a stick about four feet long and held the reins way out to one side so he couldn't jump towards me. He crouched a bit, looked at me with his big, sad eyes and took a giant leap straight towards me, like I was going to catch all 1,200 pounds of him. Water showered all over me like a water slide ride at an amusement park. I climbed on to him with my boots filled to the top with water that was now draining down through the many holes. It gave the appearance of two sprinkling cans. I tried to look nonchalant and waved at a few motorists on the highway.

I've ridden this trail several times since and someone has fixed the ledge. Versailles has about 22 miles of trails now and is a premiere place to ride. So, add it to your list for new adventures this year.

Ron and his horse Lefty at Versailles State Park in Indiana.

BETTY AND MY SQUEAKY SADDLE

NOT LONG AGO I was on one of those great Indiana Trail Riders Association-sponsored trail rides at Green Sullivan State Forest wanting to visit with as many people as I could. Eventually, I came up alongside Betty Duffy who was the ITRA director at that time. We talked a bit and I realized that she seemed somewhat annoyed about something. Finally she said that my squeaky, creaky saddle bothered her, and suggested that I either ride ahead of the group or behind the group. Personally, I like the creaky sound of my saddle; it reminds me of the Old West. So being a good guy, I brought up the rear of the group with my "rsherr ekee awaur" from my saddle being music to my ears.

Later in the camp ground I approached Betty about this, explaining that the saddle really wasn't mine. But the stirrups on this saddle were the only ones that I could adjust to my length, my wife Karen's length and our daughter Sara's length, that the purple tack wasn't mine either, and I didn't want to hear any more about it. Betty suggested that I try oiling the saddle and cleaning it up real good, but in the meantime try some baby powder on the saddle. So when I got home, I decided I'd look around for what we might have. Didn't find any baby powder but I did find some Dr. Scholl's foot powder instead. Guess that shows what age group I'm in.

I'd powdered up that saddle pretty good and tried it out. By golly! A lot of the squeaking and creaking stopped. A lot, but not all. I powdered her up again and this time got almost all the squeaks and creaks out. The third time I really powdered up the old saddle and it quieted it down just right. Problem is, now it looked like I'd been riding drag on a hundred mile cattle drive in a dry and dusty place. Shortly after that on another ride with the ITRA people, I was riding ahead of the group on my "goes anywhere, does anything horse" with that saddle, only to find those who were riding behind me laughing when I hit a trot. When I popped down in the saddle, I was leaving little clouds of white dust.

TRAIL RIDE IN PARKER, COLORADO

A BUNCH OF TRAIL RIDERS there in Parker, Colorado decided to go on a trail ride in October. Now these folks were always going on a ride, and this was back in the early 1960s. I lived on a really small ranch on the west side of Cherry Creek in Parker. I even remember a sheep herder would bring his flock onto the land north of us and would spend there a week or so. It's all condos now, so much for a lifestyle lost.

Did I ever go up and meet this sheepherder? No, because I never dreamed of such a monstrous change in lifestyle and demographics. We were all young and naïve. I guess we thought everything was going to stay the way that it was at that time. Parker had then one paved street, and as I look back on it now, all I can think is what the heck happened?

There must have been 25 or 30 riders on this ride. Some of the older ones were full of stories from the past. We rode pretty much south before turning around and coming back. There were very few gates or fences to be crossed. The first riders opened the gate and let them drop, and the last riders would close them.

At this one gate I was the last rider. That was okay I thought. I'm a self-proclaimed cowboy, so I hopped down and closed the gate. However, I encountered a great deal of difficulty in remounting as my borrowed horse really didn't want to hang around with me trying to get on. With the gate closed now, I got ready to mount up on a horse considerably taller than what I was used to, and being on the down side of the slope at that, it was a high step to try to get on.

Now that the other horses were drawing away and dropping out of my sight, things were not in my favor. I finally got my left foot in the stirrup, hopping along on my right as I couldn't pull myself up into the saddle. And my borrowed horse kept moving forward in his quest to catch up with his buddies. Finally, the land leveled out and I pulled myself up into the saddle with Dynamite, my horse, moving at a full gallop to catch up with his friends.

After a bit we came upon an old range line shack. It was pretty well built and looked comfortable. As we explored this abandoned place, I saw a calendar hanging on a wall that was dated 1942. The few notes written on it are lost in time as neither I nor anyone else recorded these few notes made by cowboys from the distant past.

As the group explored the property, an old spur was found and a couple of metal items. Too bad all of these items were not left behind where they would be more significant in the future.

Oh well, we make do with what we can and in today's world life is an adventure.

RON AND THE UMBRELLA

I LIKE TO REFERENCE THIS PERIOD OF TIME as "Back in the old days." I was the assistant manager of a chain of movie theatres in Del Rio, Texas. I guess this was about 1958 or so.

I lived fairly close to the theatre that held our offices and my day started early in the morning. I would walk to work leaving our car at home. I usually got off about 11:30 a.m., and then I was off until the drive-in theatre business started in the evening.

On this particular morning, I got ready to leave for home when I encountered something I couldn't believe. An extremely heavy rain had started. I fiddled around for a while, hoping and expecting it would let up. No such luck. I stepped out under the marquee with rain falling so hard that puddles, lakes and rivers were standing full, even on the tops of hills, and filling the streets.

Miss Ella, the head cashier, said, "You can take my umbrella and walk home." This didn't set well with me. Real men, cowboys, don't carry umbrellas. Ever seen John Wayne with one or Clint Eastwood for that matter? I stewed around for a while on this one, and Miss Ella finally said if I carried it down low, over my head, nobody would recognize me any way. After a moment I said "okay." She gave me the umbrella and I stepped out under the marquee to open it. Oh help me! It was a very large umbrella, purple in color. That was bad enough, but it was also adorned with six-inch yellow poke-a-dots. I felt committed, however, and started out, on which was basically an empty street and storefronts, devoid of people.

Holding the umbrella low over my head, I went down Main Street to where I turned off onto the street where I lived. Still nobody around. But! I forgot I had to pass the Val Verde County jail. Sure enough there was a guy there arms hanging through the bars of his cell's window. He was Mexican, probably a "wet-back," as they were called at that time, and he called out, "Hey gringo! You *'fraid* you shrink?"

That was it for me. I folded up the umbrella, got totally soaked and never carried another one for 25 years. It's funny how we can be influenced by others, even when they may be incarcerated.

LOST IN TRANQUILITY

I'M PRETTY MUCH A SPONTANEOUS TRAIL RIDER. I'll get up in the morning and suddenly decide to ride somewhere. Sometimes I'll just be puttering around the house or the barn and suddenly decide to go for a ride. Net result is that I ride a lot, but far too often by myself, which I recognize as not being a good thing to do. But if you always wait for someone to ride with, you may not get out too often.

That October day was one of those occasions. It was drop dead gorgeous outside. It was a perfect dream of a fall day. Bright sunshine, light jacket weather – I was ready. I gathered my stuff together. I left a note to Karen that I was going riding. Went over to the boarding stable where I kept my trailer, hooked up and loaded up my very much ready-to-go quarter horse, Lefty. On the 30-minute drive over to Versailles in Indiana, I sort of slipped off into a dream world, enjoying the farmland scenery and going through a couple of communities that couldn't even qualify as being small towns.

Pulling into the horseman's day use area, I found that I had the place all to myself. I took my time brushing Lefty off and saddling him while he was enjoying what was left in his hay bag. I pulled out a lawn chair and finished off my coffee from my thermos. I watched the yellow, red and gold leaves filter down from the trees as an occasional light breeze broke them loose from where they were anchored at the limbs of the trees.

I finally mounted up and rode out. I'd been riding Lefty for over 22 years and he was about as laid back a horse you'd ever want to ride. And with the total absence of horse flies, mosquitoes and other bugs local to the area at different times, I slipped off in to a magic world of just "riding along." After a while my revelry was broken with the ringing of my cell phone.

Karen, my wife, asked me where I was on the trail. Now shocked back to reality, I looked around and had absolutely no idea where I was. Now, over the years I've ridden all of the trails at Versailles many times, and now I can't determine where I'm at. Figure that one out.

Karen asked how long I'd been riding and not being sure at all I simply said with confidence "Oh, a couple of hours." She asked again where I was specifically. So I said again with confidence about halfway around the big loop. She then reminded me that we had a dinner engagement with another couple in a couple of hours. So I told her I'd be home in plenty of time.

Now was the time to assess my situation. I really didn't know where I was. To ride back from the way I came wouldn't work because it would take the same amount of time, which I figured was about two hours. So without a better plan I simply started back the way I had come when a fire service road suddenly appeared. I knew that this would bring us to the right area of the park I needed to be, so I took that path and hurried along it. Really not riding where I was supposed to but I felt this was an emergency. And it did get me back in time.

We returned to the still empty day use area. I made a high-speed return to the barn, unloaded my horse and unhooked my trailer, and arrived home with not a whole lot of time to spare.

It just goes to show you that total tranquility can get you in hot water.

THE WHO, WHEN AND WHERE

I HAVE A LOT OF PICTURES TAKEN between 1917 and 1956. All good cowboy stuff, cattle drives, people posing on horseback, some from either cattle drive camps or perhaps hunting camps.

Here's a great one. A cowboy with batwing chaps out in the middle of nowhere, riding a spotted jackass.

I'd received these pictures from my grandmother Evelyn, who is now deceased, with little or no information as to who these people are. Where or when these pictures were taken or anything else that would begin to tell the whole story is lost. Her grandfather was a pistol-toting, horseback riding Texas Ranger. So if I could put it all together the facts it could be pretty interesting.

I do feel that most of the pictures were taken in West Texas, however. The common denominator is that only six of these pictures carry any identification at all. From these six, I've been able to identify some of the other people in the other photos. So with that in mind, I know "who" in some cases, but not the "where" or "when." At one point in time in my life, I had inherited several hundred pictures from my mother and was able to go through them with her. I'd ask her why she didn't identify the "who, where and when" in the pictures, and her reply was, "Well, that's Auntie Merle, everybody knows that! That was in 1937 when she came up to visit us. Surely you remember that, don't you?" Yeah, sure mom, I was at least two when those pictures were taken.

Later, I obtained another thousand or so colored slides from my mother, none of which were labeled. By that time, my mother was far along with dementia and Alzheimer's, and those memories were lost for good. Since she was the last of that era, I had no choice but to throw them away.

So what's that got to do with trail riding? Well, maybe not that much, but it's got a lot to do with life. I had the foresight to interview my mother and my grandmother while they were both quite elderly but still sound of mind. I found out a lot. Some things sort of get swept under the rug. We even had one relative who was hung in Texas because he was a horse thief. Nobody ever wanted to talk much about that one.

I've had a lot of great trail riding experiences, and I've made a great effort to document as much of all this as I can. What a delight it is to sit down on a winters' night with a bowl of popcorn and look at all these memories. Here is one of Scotty Eskridge with a large steak looking for a fire to cook it on. I like this one of Greg Hersberger rolled back in a chair up in Salamonie Lake in Indiana. This one of Wendy Rummel when she was out here in Arizona was a reminder of a great ride. That is what it is all about, recapturing those memories and experiences. It doesn't work however without those notes as to who is in the picture and when it happened, particularly 20 years from now. Those printed pictures you can write on the back with a pencil. Don't use a pen as sometimes the ink will bleed through the picture.

Life is an adventure and those memories as seen through those pictures will last a lifetime if you can identify the *who, when* and *where.*

WHEN DO YOU BECOME TOO OLD TO RIDE?

SOME TIME AGO, I was going to one of those really great Indiana Trail Riders weekends down at Brown County State Park. I usually go down early on Friday to get an extra ride in before the events begin on Saturday morning. I had pulled in about 10:00 a.m. on a site that was along the road. While setting up camp, three couples pulled in on the opposite side of my camp. Looked to me that they might have been on the road a while as they staggered stiffly out of their rigs, but quickly they got around to their chores of setting up camp. These folks, bless their hearts, were as old as dirt. After a couple hours of chiding each other about this and that they decided to go for a ride. I watched with great fascination as two of the men took Mabel to a picnic bench then helped her onto the bench while a third person held Mabel's horse. Once on Mabel was very much in charge of a very nice looking black Walking horse. So they went, one after the other from the picnic bench onto the horse. As they rode off they were still giving each other a hard way to go about this and that. Their spirit was certainly infectious.

Along about dark here they came back very much in high spirits. They piled off their horses and the women began getting a great dinner going while the men took care of the horses. From where I was the steaks and all the trimmings looked mighty tempting to a hungry appetite. I think I even saw a little liquid refreshment on the picnic bench. Again they were kidding each other, and I was struck with the realization how much they were enjoying each other's company, the spirit of the day and riding their horses together.

Saturday morning they began to stir about and a big breakfast was in the making. Soon the dishes were cleaned up and the horses saddled. The getting on part went about the same. More ribaldry but with lunches packed and some stiffness relieved. After a night of rest their spirits were higher than ever. Off they went.

I went about my day with the ITRA with a renewed enthusiasm but was very curious about my camping neighbors. Late afternoon here they came. Their horses were sweated up and they looked like they had covered some ground. They all soon started on their various chores. With my curiosity up I had to go down and talk with one of them. I found one fella brushing down a horse and asked him how the ride had gone. He said great and that they had ridden pretty much on the west side of the camp ground. Up B trail and out to C, that's quite a ride in itself I was thinking. He went on to say they stopped for an hour or so for lunch. I had to ask about getting back on their horses to which he laughed, and said they weren't quite as agile as they once were. Mabel had a hip replacement and the others had one kind of ailment or another. He admitted that only one of them could actually mount a horse from the ground. They just look for picnic benches, high ground and stumps. For many years they had been riding together and rode fairly frequently.

What I got out of this was that they still rode, even with advanced age. These people weren't giving up riding just because they had become "old" in numbers. I'll admit it also takes a good reliable horse and there is safety in numbers. They looked out for each other, kidded each other almost constantly, and were enjoying life to the fullest. I feel they are still out there and hopefully are.

As I have become older I am a lot more careful about riding. However, being with friends, camping out and enjoying life, is the adventure life was meant to be.

So when do you become too old to ride? When the spirit leaves you.

THE BREAKING OF LEFTY

LEFTY, MY "GOES ANYWHERE, DOES ANYTHING HORSE" is mentioned in many of my stories. I only recently realized how much of an influence he had been in my life. We'd been together over 30 years, and with him becoming somewhat arthritic I didn't ride him over rough trails anymore. Nonetheless, I was still riding him until the end. I took for granted his laid back demeanor and willingness to do whatever the rider wanted.

He was born April 9, 1984 on a small piece of property that I had in Columbia, Tennessee. He was born a sorrel with a large splash of white on his forehead. He was handled a lot as a very young foal and halter broke while he was still a weanling. I had another farm of 34 acres out on the Bear Creek Pike and hauled the horses, including Lefty, in my trailer back and forth regularly. So by the time I weaned him you could easily catch him, load him in a trailer, pick up all four feet and lead him around.

Circumstances occurred in which I agreed to sell all my horses, tack, etc., and take a new job in another state. All this happened but I couldn't sell Lefty, even for $100. He was still a stud and only a yearling at this time. I was running out of time as we had sold the house and I soon had to report to work at my new job. A friend of mine who also owned Tennessee Honcho, the stud whom we had bred my quarter horse mare Diamond to, resulting in Lefty, agreed to take Lefty for a while. The farm where we took him had several hundred acres of pasture. Lefty ran out with all the other horses and cows. He was confronted with all sorts of things that horses spook from. Deer jumping up from nowhere, barking dogs, blowing trash bags, and so forth, to the point that apparently nothing much bothered him.

One day my friend called said she wanted to return my horse as he was now two and still a stud. Where should she deliver him was her next question. Hastily I found a nearby stable and shortly Lefty was delivered. He was no longer a sorrel and was black with a few gray hairs. I really don't much like black horses, second to gray or white ones. Lefty was in a stall at night and went out with the other geldings for the day. We made a gelding out of him as soon as he arrived. I was working a pretty hard schedule on my job so didn't do much with him for a couple of weeks. He seemed to be his same old self and good natured as ever. I had green broke a number of horses in the past. You know, getting the 20 rides in 30 days. I finished trained only a half dozen or so and three of them belonged to me at that.

One Saturday afternoon when I didn't have to work I got Lefty out in a round pen. Ran him around one way and stepped in front of him to reverse him and he seemed okay with that. So I tied him to the fence and sacked him out with a saddle blanket. This turned about to be a waste of time. He could have cared less. So I left it as it was and day one of training was over. I took Sunday off. Maybe I should explain: I worked seven days a week, usually 10 hours a day unless someone wanted to be off, then it was a 12-hour day.

The second time I began to work with him I spent less time on the first step segments, just sacking him out briefly. Then I saddled him and then ran him around some in the round pen. I don't know why, but I put a bridle on him with a low curb bit. He chewed on that for a while and then, for no reason, I just got on him. No preliminary step up with a little weight or anything like that. Just climbed on and walked him around the round pen for a while. He did chew on the bit for quite a while. I got off, unsaddled and really brushed him down.

Lefty influenced me many times over the years, changing my personal life. One of the first influences was that Lefty gave me the horsemanship opportunity I had always sought after. I'm not the big city, condo-living person some people tried to make me. My feelings for Lefty were boundless and he made me feel real.

Shortly after that, one day after work, I repeated the same process and was riding Lefty when two other boarders at the stable, young women I might add, said they were riding out and would cross the Little Miami River and be gone only an hour or so. Did I want to come along? Sure, why not? Lefty followed along, seemingly enjoying the change in scenery. At the river crossing where I expected to turn around to return Lefty just followed the other two, sloshing water for a moment with his front feet, getting himself and rider wet. We moved along the trail on the other side, trotting some. I was in seventh heaven. The return crossing on the river was also uneventful.

I'd probably never do that ride again with such a green horse but really felt I was on top of the world with such an outstanding trail horse. I knew I would never sell him and he would become my connection to country life while others tried to make me a city boy. Soon my kids and others were riding Lefty while I rode a friend of mine's horse.

Had it not been for Lefty and his "goes anywhere, does anything" approach to life, I'd never come to know one of those two girls I made that first ride with. Karen and I shared so many rides together after that. It was inevitable that we would fall in love, and through thick and thin get married. All of these positive things I attribute to my friend, Lefty.

RATTLESNAKE CANYON

We were down at the Prude Guest Ranch just outside Fort Davis, Texas enjoying its pleasant surroundings. The weather is always great, especially in the summer as the ranch is at about 5000 feet. My grandmother Evelyn had married John Prude —the ranch owner— later in life, and had asked us to come down for another visit. We had always enjoyed their company and staying at the ranch. The ranch's 42 Southwestern style family cabins had always been a treat. The cabins all have porches for guests to sit on which is nice, especially in the evenings when the stars are really brilliant.

John didn't have phones in the rooms or TVs. His theory being that if all guests wanted to do was watch TV or talk on the phone they might as well stay home. There are however two recreation rooms that do have TVs along with fireplaces. The food at the dining hall that seats 150 is absolutely unparalleled and the spacious dining room is filled with character. I had always liked to go on a trail ride in the morning followed up with a dip in the indoor pool. With great views, western riding and fabulous food, this is great place to be for a vacation without the hassle that most of us take for granted. If you get a chance check out their website at: prude-ranch.com. They have a summer program for kids from June 8th to August 2nd, so things are a little bit more active during that period of time.

This type of relaxed atmosphere found a bunch of us down at the dining hall on the last night of my visit. I had to be in Dallas the next day so I was savoring the surroundings along with the last of some leftover Peach Cobbler. John clanked in still wearing his spurs after a day of riding, announcing that he needed to roundup all the horses the next morning as there was a fella that wanted to pick out a few to break. He asked if any of us wanted to ride along. Needless to say, any thought of being in Dallas the next day quickly evaporated. We all wanted to be in this roundup which I knew would cover about 4000 acres of ground, and we agreed to meet right after breakfast ready to ride.

The next morning after breakfast I headed down to the corrals with the other riders to get saddled up. There were two couples from Fort Worth that were mounted up on four of the sharpest cutting horses I've seen in a long time. They had been on the road participating in a couple of cutting competitions, and had stopped at the Prude Ranch to rest up for a couple of days and enjoy a little trail riding before going home. The other riders were two cowboys who worked on the ranch and were mounted on a couple of the ranch's best horses. Of course, John was riding his Palomino Gelding, Golden Dude, which he had been riding forever. The horse selected for me came out of the Dude's string, a pinto named Fat Albert. That's what the wranglers called him. He looked the part too.

John gave us a few instructions and we set off at a fast walk. When we stopped, John sent the first couple off and had one of the cowboys go along just in case they needed anything, and to make sure they didn't get lost. John told them to be sure not to miss several scenic views along the way. The rest of us took off at a high trot and slow lope. Stopping after a bit John dropped the other couple off, telling them to ride up on a bluff to see some beautiful views, and also which direction to drive any horses they might find. Of course, he sent the other cowboy along for the same reasons he sent the first one. We really took off then and I'll admit Fat Albert did really good at a high lope. I glanced over to look at John, gray hair streaming out from under his hat and a hint of tears in his eyes from the cold wind whipping in. You would never have guessed he was eighty plus years old. We stopped and he told me to ride up on a mesa, round up all the horses I could find, and head them down Rattlesnake Canyon, which he pointed out to me. "Are there any rattlesnakes in there?" I asked. He replied, "Well, when you get to the top of the canyon and start down, you might want to push any stock you've found into a gallop," and off he went. No mention of beautiful views, no cowboy helper to make sure I didn't get lost.

It was just up to Albert and me. I did find a couple of horses up on the mesa and as I headed to the top of rattlesnake canyon, I found some more horses, giving me seven to herd to the valley. I really pushed the seven down the canyon and found it was pretty narrow. My clouded mind saw snakes on shelves about eyeball height lying in wait to get me. There weren't any, however, as my imagination was running wild.

We all got to the valley about the same time with a hundred or so horses that made quite a sight doing a slow gallop towards the corrals. It was a "Kodak moment" if there was ever one, but I had no choice but to keep going or be totally left behind. The horses seem to know where they were going and were soon into the corrals.

We all had lunch with the sensation of great accomplishment. I had never been on a roundup of any kind up to that day so I was really exuberant over this experience. We were left to wondering how many people working in a factory or high rise office would have exchanged places with us that morning. Maybe it's time to check out that website?

JOHN SELLING HORSE

KIND OF A LONG STORY HERE so I'll shave it off a bit. My grandmother, Evelyn Poag, married John Prude, a west Texas rancher, some ten years after my maternal grandfather died. John then owned and ran the Prude Guest Ranch in Fort Davis, Texas. He was quite a character, guest ranch owner, college professor, and already the world's best optimist that I have ever met. Everything works out as these two stories will tell.

Karen and I were visiting at the ranch several years ago. We were treated to one of the 42 cabins on the ranch. But the place I liked most was the screened-in front porch of John and Evelyn's house on the ranch. John and I were sitting there one morning discussing all kinds of really important things, cattle prices, rain, stock tanks and range conditions, when the phone rang.

John took the call and a short time later said to me, "Ronald, (he always called me Ronald) that was a fellow from Dallas, he said his young son was here for our summer children's program and really fell in love with the horse he was assigned, Cherokee. He said he would give me $1,000 for the horse and pick it up on Saturday. What do you think of this?"

After some moments of thought I told him to sell Cherokee. It would make a young kid very happy, the horse would enjoy going to a different home and not be in a dude string, and moving on to a one-on-one relationship with his rider.

John indicated that this horse was the best he had in the dude string but he would do it. And so he called the Dallas fellow back. I could see that John was really thinking about all of this as we sat on the porch and as he was pretty quiet. The phone rang again and he answered. After a short conversation he said we would have to take the trailer and go to town for few minutes.

It seemed that a young man from Fort Davis was getting ready to go to college and needed to sell his favorite horse, Rusty, for some much needed income. Said he would take $500 for it. So John, without the blink of an eye, had agreed. And then he said to me, "Ronald, I know that horse Rusty, and that horse is 100 percent better than Cherokee." When you are an eternal optimist, things just seem to come out okay – most of the time.

Here's another positive thinking story. I want to add this one, again, expounding on John's optimism.

John and Evelyn had travelled to a very remote ranch in West Texas as John was looking for some needed horses for his guest string. They accomplished this and set about their trip about home. They were going along, basically on a two-track road, very seldom used, miles from anywhere and no cell phone contact. Dang if they just didn't have a flat tire there right in the middle of the two tracks! John, who was in his mid-80s, did not have the physical ability to change the tire. Grandmother Evelyn, becoming very emotional and upset said, "We'll die here! Nobody ever comes by here for weeks at a time."

John on the other hand was wringing his hands with the anticipation that "We are going to meet somebody new today." Well, sure enough, along came a cowpuncher in a rattling old pick-up truck. As he set about changing the tire, John was all over him with questions. Cattle prices holding up? Water tanks dry or grass holding up okay? Having to move cattle a lot just for feed? Horses holding up? He was so excited about meeting this guy who had a lot of information.

John told him they could meet up in the next town where he'd buy lunch for him, and they would catch up on the ranching activities in this area. John had made another one of many new friends in his life.

JOHN'S BLACK BEAR

I WAS LUCKY A NUMBER OF YEARS AGO to go on a few horse rides with my step-grandfather, John G. Prude. His father had started the Prude Guest Ranch quite a number of years previously in Fort Davis, Texas. This guest ranch boasted having 30 RV hook up sites, a spacious ranch dining room, and an indoor pool.

The ranch was established in 1896 by Andrew G. Prude. In the mid-1930s, the family decided to add accommodations and services as a guest ranch to offset the income loss on cattle due to drought conditions. Upon Andrew's passing, John G. Prude, his son, became the second generation to run the ranch. With his skill and guidance the guest activities were greatly expanded. During the 1950s, the children's summer camping program was added to the ranch activities. John G. Prude passed away in February of 2000, and therefore his son John Robert Prude, became the third generation to run the ranch.

The ranch has had a vast number of well-known people over the years, my favorite being the writer J. Frank Dobie. He wrote a tribute of his visit in an inscription of a book which I now have. He commented sitting in one of the chairs in the lodge about the view that he had, and the wild turkeys he saw. I have rested in the same chair in that lodge, and it has become an experience I greatly cherish.

The Prude Ranch is filled with historical memories, and an indescribably true western lifestyle sets the stage for an experience that

I had with John on one of our several rides together. We had ridden out from the ranch to go to a windmill to check the water levels. John pointed out as we rode along at what looked to me like a cedar tree, and said, "Now remember this tree and where it is." Soon we came upon an old windmill still pumping its water into the stock tank. He then related this story.

Back in the 1930s, during the Great Depression, the Government formed the CCC (Civilian Conservation Corps). They had sent out three of their workers to construct this very windmill and pump. One day, while they were pretty well along with the project, a very large aggressive black bear appeared on the scene. The three CCC fellows quickly ascended the windmill tower. After a time, with the bear still hanging around, two of them decided they would distract the bear, while the third fellow would run to the Prude Ranch for help. They pulled this off without incident.

Upon arriving at the ranch, the third fellow told John what had happened. John quickly saddled his number one horse, Comanche, and rode to the other two fellows' rescue. Sure enough, they were still up in the windmill with the bear growling at them below. John whipped out his lariat and quickly roped the bear. Unfortunately, he roped not around his neck, but around his body just behind his forelegs. About this time John, his horse and the bear all took off. They came to this tree John had pointed out to me earlier in that day. The bear went to one side, Comanche and John to the other. When the rope tightened they were going full speed past one another, and after completing the full circle, they passed each other again. About this time, Comanche had enough of all of this, and the lariat slipped from the saddle horn. Comanche decided that the best thing to do was go home in a hurry with John still on board.

The CCC people were contacted about these happenings and arrived on the scene and captured the bear who had still been tied to the tree. They put him in a cage and took him to their camp. There they treated the bear as a pet. One morning, about 4:00 a.m. or so, the CCC camp's cook arrived in the cookhouse, which was very poorly lit, to fix breakfast for the crew. He heard some shuffling around in the kitchen and couldn't figure out what it was. That is, until the bear reared up on its hind legs, so according to John that's the last they ever saw of him – the cook that is. The Superintendent had enough of all of this and crated the bear up and sent him to the San Antonio Zoo.

Many claim today that any of the black bears that you see in the zoo today are descended from him.

Ron and Jonathan pushing the main herd at Saddle Rock Ranch. Holbrook, Arizona on October 1, 2002.

Board Meeting at the Saddle Rock Ranch. From left to right: Al Spall, Warren Simmons, and Ranch owner Ray Deskins. May 12, 2003.

THE SADDLE ROCK RANCH

An invitation was offered to me to participate in a cattle drive on the Saddle Rock Ranch up in the Holbrook, Arizona area. I sure jumped on this opportunity.

The Saddle Rock Ranch is so named due to a 20-foot tall rock formation shaped like a saddle that is alongside the drive way leading to the ranch headquarters. An enterprising soul placed a coil of barbwire about six feet in diameter over the saddle horn. Sure looks real.

The ranch is on the west side of Highway 180 and is located across from the Petrified Forest National Park. Our main job was to gather all the stock on some 13 sections of land, and drive them under a bridge on Highway 180. In this group were ranch owner Ray, ranch manager "Pencil Head" Bart, and old timer Warren, all of these men having a lot of experience. For the rest of us this was a somewhat new experience. We spread out on a line about three miles wide and worked our way north. The land here is fairly flat with numerous outcroppings of rock and many dry washes. Ray had taken a moment with me and pointed to where the bridge underpass was. Everything kind of blended together as I rode on, and really didn't have any landmarks to keep me and Lefty on the right track.

We continued to gather cows, bulls and calves until we had about 200 head as we neared the highway. I then saw "Pencil Head" Bart on a bluff looking like John Wayne. Being a big man himself, with a tall high crowned hat. He was waving his hand and hollering, "Bring 'em on boys!" We came upon an arroyo that ran under the bridge, only to find the fence had no gate, and I realized we were entirely in the wrong place. We were about one mile too far south. By the time we as a group realized our mistake, the herd had continued to drift south. Two riders got out in front of them and turned 'em back north. I was riding on the flank.

The drag riders were hollering to keep up the pressure and keep them along the fence. I knew what would happen as soon as they hit the arroyo. They wouldn't go across but would break west in the arroyo. I wasn't riding enough horse to get into a header position. And the others were really pushing the cattle at a full run.

When we got to the arroyo, that's exactly what the herd did. They ran left and west. The wash had created a three-foot high ledge of sand and dirt which I came upon at a full lope. Lefty, my "goes anywhere does anything horse" slammed on the brakes but crashed over the ledge anyway. I couldn't believe he landed on all four feet.

Now I was in front of the slowing herd and with some help from another rider got them strung out along the fence, headed north and ultimately through the open gate. Temperatures were good up there in the high country, and I wore a sweatshirt all day. The wind, however, was 30 miles per hour, laced with sand which made the seven-mile ride back to the ranch headquarters uncomfortable. The chuck at the ranch was something to crow about.

I'm looking forward to doing this again.

DUMPED IN CACTUS

It was in the early fall back in the 1960s when my family and I lived on a small ranch in Colorado with another young couple, Ray and Sharon. They had invited some friends out for a ride and a barbecue, even borrowed my horse so that they all could ride on that Sunday afternoon. Before long they all got going having a great time riding here and there, whooping and hollering on this really nice Colorado fall afternoon.

I was watching from my living room picture window when this one young woman's horse just broke in half, sending her skyward spinning around like a helicopter, with one hand groping down for a long-gone saddle horn. She came down "whump" in the middle of the biggest clump of prickly pear cactus on the whole ranch. Everyone was suddenly running around like a bunch of chickens trying to see what happened and what to do next.

Sharon apparently figured it out and ran to my door. "We need your station wagon to get her to the hospital." We folded the seats down and loaded her in on her tummy. I'd never seen so many cactus thorns stuck in anybody. Sharon had rushed to her house and got a pair of tweezers. She then climbed in the back of my station wagon pulling out prickly pear thorns, as I hastily pulled out of my driveway headed for the hospital.

When the three of us arrived at the hospital and pulled up to the emergency room, the attendants rushed out with a gurney, and Sharon and I really got going on pulling out those thorns out as they rolled her into the emergency room. This young woman who was 23 or 24 was in a great deal of pain, and a doctor came out and gave her a shot of something that put her off into never-never land.

In the private emergency room that we were given, a very authoritative nurse who Sharon and I called "Miss Smug and Correct," gave us two five-inch long stainless steel tweezers, and we really got going pulling thorns out. Sharon would say, "Help me with this one, it's broke off at the skin." Or I would say, "Squeeze this area here." The nurse in charge of everything came in and told us to get her T-shirt and jeans off. We got this done and encountered a whole new crop of deeply embedded prickly pear thorns. We proceeded to do our best to get these thorns out. Now "Miss Nurse who has everything under control" came in and said, "We need to get those undergarments off." Sharon looked at me and I looked at her, and wordlessly we did just that and continued to pull thorns. We really worked well together making sure all areas were checked for thorns on this now naked girl, extracting thorns by the dozens.

Another nurse stuck her head in the door and addressed "Miss I've got everything under control nurse," saying, "This girl's husband wants to know how she's doing." "Miss Perfect Nurse" looked at me with her eyes beginning to relentlessly cross, realizing that something wasn't under her area of perfect control.

"Whooo, whoo are you?" Finally came out of her strangled sounded mouth. I told her simply that I had brought her here and said, "I've never met this girl and I don't even know her name." She answered, "Out!!!" With her finger and hand jabbing furiously in the air, her eyes crossing relentlessly with a total loss of control, and I realized she was close to a total breakdown.

I handed her my tweezers and humbly said, "I was only trying to help."

THE SECOND LONG HORN ROUNDUP

WHEN IT COMES TO CATTLE ROUNDUPS, I really prefer not to have a job. Although I really enjoy the riding part and the gathering of cattle, but it can be demanding. If you are not riding enough horse, stock can slip past you, and then you feel you are not up to the real cowboy standards. I like being retired. Just taking pictures and finding something to write about keeps me plenty occupied.

The first round up was in November, and we had hoped to gather all the stock running on some nine sections of rangeland. Some stock was missed, however, and some of the calves were too small to be "worked." The second round up was scheduled for early spring, but rain came big time and the roundup was cancelled.

Can't really be effective branding in wet weather as the wet hair cools the branding iron too much to get the job done right. The next try for a roundup came on March 7th, 2015 at the Don Donnelly's D-Spur Ranch in Gold Canyon, AZ. I had maintained a low profile hoping my boss Shelly wouldn't have a job for me. No such luck there. She asked me to be the gateman. I didn't know if I should ask what a gate man does or not. I didn't want to appear to be too dumb, so I didn't ask.

On the day of the roundup the weather was extraordinarily nice, a cool 72 degrees and a clear sky. Twenty-seven riders showed up for this exciting experience. I don't know the actual status but seven or eight of them were very experienced. Another seven or eight had done this kind of thing before, and for the rest it was a relatively new experience.

They set off on time and we expected them back by lunch. I now found that there was another gateman who knew exactly what to do. When the riders pushed their gather into a trap, which was a triangular shaped pen with an opening of a couple hundred feet at one end, the riders would hold the stock at that opening and the gatemen, on foot, would take over. Driving the stock into the end of the triangle to a solidly built catch pen, this whole triangular shaped pen was fenced with four strands of bob-wire and saguaro cactus ribs laced through the strands every two or three inches.

When working cattle on foot, you always look for a fence to use as an escape route, you know, just in case... This fence didn't offer that kind of an escape route whatsoever. The palo verde trees growing in the trap weren't too big and were the kind that had those big, nasty thorns. Before long, here came ten or so cows and steers. They were being herded along by three or four riders. All went very well and the other gateman (Bill) referred to our job as being "shushers" as in shoo cow shoo. They moved right along into the catch pen where we snapped closed the big iron gate.

Then we called out the ear tag numbers to the boss. After that, we opened the side gate and *shushered* the stock into the big corral. We had a few more groups of stock which we handled the same way, and I was impressed with how smoothly it all went.

Then, here came one all by itself. I recognized him as being the herd bull and he was not a happy camper. All of the other stock has walked or just ambled in. The bull, however, was at a trot. He went to the end near the catch pen but would not go in. My *shusher* partner and I advanced towards him. I was armed only with a saguaro rib about three-feet long that was rotten enough to keep crumbling away in my hand. My fellow *shusher* was equipped with an only less rotten stick.

This bull weighed about 2,000 pounds and has a horn span nearing seven feet. He stood at the catch pen gate nervously glaring at us. He with his front hoof caught up a big clod of dirt and threw it up over his shoulder. With a big bawl, lowered his head and started at a trot straight for me! We both started hollering, we raised our arms up over our heads and waved them frantically. The bull returned down to the catch pen to the other end of the trap. I began to realize that this may not be a good time to be a *shusher*, being armed only with about one foot of rotten saguaro rib. And with a fence that is often referred to a cowboy's best friend, which was not friendly at all.

The bull had different ideas about this whole process and decided to go back outside to the pasture where it was nice and quiet. Again he took an ambling walk towards us. We again started waving our arms and tried to make ourselves look as large as we could and advance menacingly towards him. The bull stopped and seemed confused by not just one person but two coming towards him. And he went back and eventually went into the trap, and we snapped the gate closed on him. My voice was kind of squeaky now and I was not able to call out the ear tag number, but the boss knew which bull it was.

Lunch was served around noon that day when all the stock had been driven in. We had large quantities of chili, beans, coleslaw, cake, salad, iced tea and water. We sat out under a big tent and listened to the music of a live cowboy band, and I found that I was still alive!

Then Indiana Governor Mike Pence with Ron awarding him membership to TAASOSPSB.

TAASOSPSB

THIS IS THE ACRONYM OF A REALLY FINE ORGANIZATION in which if you belong has no strings attached. This is how the "American Amalgamated Society of Semi-Professional Saddle Bums" came about.

Some time ago I had asked Indiana Trail Riders Association Director, Betty Duffy, to do something for us. She said she'd take care of it, and gave me her business card with her phone number in case I needed to contact her. I noticed the card read "Betty Duffy, Professional Trail Rider." Boy, did I like the sound of that.

I somewhat jokingly said to her that I ride a lot and camp with my horse, so can I claim to be a professional trail rider? She smiled and with a knowing look said she would send me the requirements. She did; the requirements she outlined are at the end of this story. Turns out she had done all of that and I couldn't measure up at all. I was somewhat miffed and crushed. At the next ITRA gathering, I expressed my disappointment to my buddies, Scotty Eskridge and Greg Hersberger.

Scotty said, "Well, we must be at least semi-professional," and Greg said, "Why don't we start a semi-professional group?" We then made up a very nice eight-by-eleven certificate, and gave ourselves prestigious positions over which we sign our names. To make things easy for ourselves, however, we have no meetings, no rules, no board of directors, no by-laws, and no treasury. We don't even keep track of the membership.

We do, however, as in professional baseball and other sport groups, pay our members each year a salary.

Now in the sports world the professionals get the big bucks. Meaning hundreds of thousands or more a year; whereas the semiprofessionals get considerably less. Now, Betty won't disclose how much she makes, but I can guess as you can too. So accordingly, we pay 25 cents per year, paid annually at the Hoosier Horse Fair if you can find one of us there. A recent inductee was former Indiana governor, Mike Pence. I explained to him that I felt that this was Indiana's answer to a Kentucky Colonel. We'll see if he picks up on this outstanding opportunity.

Then Governor Pence did ask where all the money came from for salaries as he is ever conscious of a balanced budget. I explained I found a $20 bill in a Kroger's parking lot, and since most members can't find us at the Hoosier Horse Fair, we are still in good financial shape.

So you consider yourself a professional trail rider? Here's a list of criteria. See how you measure up:

- Minimum of six weeks on the road with your own horse
- Travel at least 10,000 miles/year with your horse in tow
- Spend at least three hundred hours a year in the saddle
- Travel to places across the Mississippi River
- Ride in four national forests on your own horse
- Ride in a least one national park on your own horse
- Ride in at least three state forests on your own horse
- Ride in a minimum of ten states on your own horse
- Ride a horse in a minimum of eight states
- Ride a horse outside the 48 contiguous states
- Ride along an ocean

- Take at least one moonlight ride per year on your own horse

- Ride at least three horses that do not belong to you or anyone in your immediate family

- Volunteer as an Officer or Director of at least one organization that promotes trail riding for a minimum of five years

- Attend at least two seminars per year regarding horse care or trail education

- Volunteer at your state horse fair for at least one entire day

TAASOSPSB membership certificate. May 18, 2013.

The American Amalgamated Society of Semi-Profesional Saddle Bums

Hereby certifies that

_____

is a member of this prestigious national organization of semi-professional trail riders in good standing and even when in shaky standing which sometimes occurs.

As of this date

_____

| *Ron McCoy* | *Scotty E. Schmidt* | *Shey Hereby* |
| Primary Founder and Senior Executive Officer of Operations | Co-Founder and Senior Board Chairman | 1st Founder, President and Active Senior Officer |

UNINVITED DINNER GUEST

THE WEATHER WAS BECOMING HOT, 103 degrees that Sunday. In the evening, when it had become cooler, I embarked on one of my favorite activities: grilling out. I fixed some really big burgers for the grill and estimated they were 1/3 pounders. Biggies, spruced up with onions, eggs and seasoning, and my special sauce.

When I got them cooked, we went inside to eat as it was quite a bit cooler in the AC. As we sat down to eat, I looked out our sliding glass door window and saw a big bob cat walking along the top of our patio wall.

The evening sun shone on him illuminating his tawny hair and varied markings. Needless to say, he was headed for the grill. Karen, our dog Teddy, and I looked like The Three Stooges admiring the bobcat, while at the same time scrambling for the camera, or camcorder or anything while trying to keep this bobcat in sight. Dog Teddy was frantic to go outside as he was looking for a new friend, and the bobcat was looking for something in lieu of hamburgers.

When we stepped out to the patio, the bobcat dropped over the wall into our neighbor's backyard. With some more Three Stooges' activity, Karen and I looked for something to stand on to see over the seven-foot wall. Now we got some pictures of him sauntering along the neighbor's yard. Then he made a dash towards the front of the neighbor's house. We scrambled again falling over one another to go out the front door. Yep, he was there lying at the corner of the neighbor's house. After we took a couple pictures of him something unusual happened. A young woman came by walking her dog and talking on her cell phone, completely oblivious of why we were standing in the middle of the street taking pictures. So much for the marvels of the electronic age.

Since the pictures we took of the bobcat just weren't exciting, I decided that I would slip around him and chase him up the wildlife corridor. He wasn't buying that and went back to the seven-foot wall of the neighbor's backyard. And with absolutely no effort whatsoever sprang to the top and over. We got a few more pictures of him getting a drink out of the neighbor's swimming pool and then disappeared into the wildlife corridor behind our house.

Later that evening as dusk really began to creep in, I was lounging in a patio chair and watching our dog, Teddy, in our backyard. I became uncomfortable and I realized that something was watching me. As I looked about over the patio I became aware of two eyes, two ears and a nose staring at me over the concrete back wall between our neighbor and us.

PICKING UP TRASH HAS SOME HAZARDS

My first introduction to the Indiana Trail Riders Association came on a cleanup ride at Brown County State Park in Indiana. This was back some 20 years ago. Back then, it was not unusual to collect a couple of pick-up loads of trash we had picked up along the trails. It's a lot less now for probably two reasons. We've begun making major inroads in educating the public not to dump trash out on the trails and have put a lot of time and effort cleaning up along those trails.

The cleanup riders come in two categories. Trash pickers armed with a stick with a serrated nail on the end of the stick and the point sharpened, which is great for stabbing and returning cans and paper without having to get off your horse. If you're with a group that's large enough, there might be someone riding behind you to carry off everything you've picked up off the trail. Another rider would be equipped with a stick with an L-shaped nail used to retrieve bottles, although we don't see too many bottles.

The second is an elite group called "Chainsaw Gang." They have to be certified by the state to operate a chainsaw on state property. This group is frequently called into action by various property managers every time a heavy wind storm comes along. I understand their pride in their work as they are very well equipped to quickly and safely clear trails. I myself never advanced to this high level of work doing my best as a "picker" getting cans.

I really enjoy riding along, relaxed, and occasionally snapping up a can or piece of paper. This does not occur without an occasional incident. My close friend and buddy, Greg Hersberger and I, were riding along in front, in charge, being the main pickers. Sometimes a piece of trash might be found pretty far off the trail in an awkward spot. And we'd have to dismount to retrieve it. Greg almost always dismounted deferring to me and my age. On this one occasion he didn't do that. Just said, "I'll hold your horse." I didn't see the can to be picked up and he was guiding me with a "take a couple steps to the left and two more straight ahead." "Hey, Greg," I responded, "I still don't see it." With some exasperation in his voice he said, "It's about five feet in front of you right in the middle of that big clump of poison ivy you're standing in."

ROUNDUP INTERRUPTION

While working at one of the D-Spur roundups as a gateman, I observed this somewhat unusual incident. I could not hear any of the conversation, but from these people's actions and interactions with people I've encountered on the range, this is how I perceived it as I really don't know what happened at this point. But from my limited vision it could have gone like this:

The cattle were being driven in to the catch pens by the cowboys and cowgirls, a few at a time, so I was only occasionally busy at the trap.

I was looking out over the range for the next bunch of cattle to come in. To my surprise I saw seven or eight ATVs in a neat line going over to where the cowboys had gathered a sizeable bunch of cattle.

One of the ATVs likely occupied by "Push Rod" Klincker and his girlfriend Maudy were edging out from the group when they saw the cattle. I can only assume what they were saying, and I can only judge by their actions what their conversation might have been.

Maudy was pointing at them and probably said something like, "Look at all those cows." "Push Rod" likely responded, "Those are all steers or bulls. They are like deer and the males have horns that they lose in the fall. You know, like deer and elk." Maudy, likely gushed over what "Push Rod" had said and replied, "Oh Push Rod, you're so cool! And you know so much about nature!" "Push Rod" likely would have answered with, "Just because I was raised in the big city don't mean I don't know what's going on out here in the wild. Get that camcorder out! And we'll go down there and get some pictures. Folks back in the big city will never believe this." Maudy fished out the camcorder. "Push Rod, you're so wonderful at this adventure!"

While the other ATV folks looked at each other, they remained where they were. "Push Rod" and Maudy drove down into the middle of the herd. "Wow! Look at this!" Exclaimed "Push Rod" as the herd split in every direction imaginable. "Look at those bulls jumping over the bushes," called Push Rod. Maudy said, "This is so neat, Push Rod! You're the greatest!" "Oh my gosh, one is trying to hook the front of our four-wheeler! Tell him he can't do that!" Cried out Maudy. About that time Maudy exclaimed, "Oh! Look there is a cowboy over there. Do you see him? Oh my gosh, he's got a gun in his hand! He is pointing it right at us!"

Get this b@#!*# thing going you dumb s#!*&! How stupid s@#*% can you be?

Next, I saw seven or eight ATVs spread out across the hillside going as fast as they could in the direction they had come.

SUITCASE SURPRISE

IT WAS A WARM, SUNNY FALL AFTERNOON in Middle Tennessee. The sun brought the color of the yellow and golden leaves to a brilliant highlight as they filtered down from the high above tree limbs. Claud and Clovis were walking out in the woods for the pure enjoy moment of crunching through the leaves and just being in the great outdoors.

As they ambled along the seldom used two-track country lane they came upon a deep ravine where locals —thinking they were doing a great deed— dumped their trash. Unfortunately this was a fairly common practice in that part of the country. Claud and Clovis looked at the mess and checked it out. A bird cage, refrigerator, mattress, an old suitcase and just about everything else. Shortly the two guys continued on their way when they heard a "Yowell." "What's that?" Clovis said. "I don't know," Claud replied. About that time they heard it again. Claud said, "Let's drift over that way."

Soon they came across a huge bobcat caught in a trap. Clovis excitedly claimed, "Wow! I can see him stuffed by my fireplace. Teeth bared and one paw reaching up." Claud eagerly agreed with his vision. Now, like most good old boys in that part of the country, they carried a small can of anesthesia to put a captured animal to sleep to release it from a trap without damaging a potential pelt. Clovis squirted a couple of times with the anesthesia and the bobcat plopped right over sound asleep. Claud released him and said, "How are we going to get him home?" Clovis replied, "Let's go back to that dump. Maybe that bird cage will work." Back they went.

The bird cage was too beat up, but that suitcase was just right. So they picked up the bobcat, put him in the suitcase and were soon headed out to the old Bear Creek Highway.

About the time they got to their truck, Clovis had second thoughts. "Claud, I can't kill the bobcat. And I don't think the wife will like him by the fireplace either. Claud, do you want him?" Claud replied, "No, not me." "What should we do now?" Clovis asked, as they approached the highway. "I know! We'll just set the suitcase handle up right at the edge of the highway," was his reply.

They did this and on returning to the parked truck Clovis asked, "What now?" Claud's answer was, "Why don't we sit in the truck and see what happens."

Several cars and trucks ripped by paying no attention to the suitcase. Then, here it came, an old Cadillac with those big fins and an Alabama license plate. Through the back windows all you could see were heads, arms and legs. The car looked like it was collapsed on the pavement as the taillights winked on. The back door opened. An arm reached out and snatched the suitcase up. Then the old Cadillac roared off, blue smoke rolling from its spinning tires.

Claud and Clovis looked at each other. "Let's go after them!"

The old Cadillac had picked up quite a bit of speed when suddenly the brake lights came up with unprecedented brilliance and again, blue smoke rolled out from all four tires as the wheels locked up, and the car slid down the highway. All four doors snapped open and people exploded out.

The next day, headlines on the Columbia Herald Tribune: "Carver Family Routed From Automobile by 'Suitcase Surprise'."

WHAT WUZ THAT?

MY BUDDY, LOU SAMPSON, TELLS US THIS STORY: He and a bunch of good ole boys from Middle Tennessee set up a "coon" hunt up near Fort Knox, Kentucky. Raccoons being a nocturnal critter made this a night hunt. They all showed up on the appointed night, some eight to nine of them. All ready to go out on a hunt and bringing with them some 12 to 16 coonhounds.

The night closed in and despite some threatening, rainy weather, they set off in high spirits. Shining their lights up into the trees, looking this way and that, dogs were leading the way bellowing and baying. They knew this was going to be a great hunt.

Then a light rain began, and the boys broke out their ponchos and assorted rain gear. Their resolve was only slightly dampened. Around midnight, however, the skies really opened up. One fellow said, "I know of an old shotgun cabin up ahead. Let's hole up there for a spell." Sure enough it was just ahead.

Now a shotgun cabin was generally built in the early 1900s, and consisted of two rooms with a wall and a doorway dividing the two rooms. This cabin's roof was caved-in in the middle, but they had shelter around the edges. A lantern was placed in the doorway between the two rooms. The boys and dogs settled down in one room relaxing, not saying much, and partaking in some adult liquid refreshments.

Suddenly, something wasn't right. The dogs went on high alert but remained quiet. The terrible stench of death filled their nostrils. And they all sensed a presence. Looking at the doorway they saw a great, hairy monster. Long hair covered its head and shoulders. Two glowing, penetrating yellow eyes stared at them when suddenly it kicked over the lantern, immediately plunging the cabin into total blackness. In the same instance, all the boys ran out of the door all at the same time with the now panicked, scrambling hounds scrambling over the top of them with lightning speed.

Lou said he went a quarter of a mile before he could even get his feet to touch the ground. Back at their trucks the dogs couldn't get into the safety of their transportation boxes quick enough. The hunters got into their trucks without a word and waited for morning.

Daylight came to an overcast sky, light rain falling and a foggy mist covered the area. They all got out of their trucks and wordlessly looked at each other. One of them said, "Let's get started and go back to get our guns and other stuff back there." Another fellow who was drawing circles in the gravel with his toe started, "Well, I told Mabel I'd be home early to help with the ironing," and with that he and his buddy climbed in their truck and left. Another good ole boy looking confused said he was leaving also. When questioned about his new 12-gauge shotgun he said with some scorn, "Well, that gun's not much account. You guys can have it if you want." With that he climbed in his truck and disappeared down the road.

With about half of them already gone, the others decided to head back to the shotgun cabin, unarmed at that. The mist and light fog didn't add to their confidence. Approaching the cabin with cautious half-steps and stops they suddenly saw him: "It was a billy goat." There he was grazing on the grass.

As some of you may know, when frightened or disturbed, a billy goat will rise up on their hind legs giving the impression of a great hairy monster.

HOW MUCH WILL A HORSE COST ME?

THIS QUESTION WAS ASKED OF ME BACK IN A TIME I refer to as the "olden days," the 1960s. I was working at my desk in the equipment planning office at Beech Aircraft. An attractive young woman approached my desk with a "peck, peck, peck" ringing from her high heels.

"Hi!" She said. "I'm told you have horses and know all about them." I responded with a modest "I've got a few. Don't know about the 'knows all about them' part, however." Then she offered her reason for her visit. "I really want a horse and need to know how much one would cost me. What do you think?"

After a moment of thought I told her about $40,000. I heard her gasp and saw disbelief in her eyes. She spun on those little high heels and left without a word, and I could only hear the peck, peck of those heels.

Oh, oh, I knew I had hit a nerve.

A month later or so I heard a high-heeled sound and here she comes again. Stopped in front of my desk, cocked one hip and put her hand on it. "Well, Mr. Smarty Pants, I got a horse and only spent $200 for it." That's great," I said, "get some tack." She responded that she got a used saddle and bridle and a new saddle blanket. "Hope you didn't have to spend too much." "Ran about $300, but really nice stuff." "Get out and ride," I offered with a smile.

Some three months later, I heard the high heels headed my way. She rested her two hands on the edge of my desk and said that she and her husband were enjoying her horse so much that they bought one for him. Spent all their time riding now. She smiled and disappeared down the hall. It was indicated this time, however, that the second horse and tack cost about the same as the first.

A little more time passed and I had gone to a gymkhana in a nearby town. I wasn't too surprised to see her there. She came over to me and told me her husband had traded off his car for a new truck. And a friend of theirs had sold them a nice used horse trailer. "Wow, that's great," was all I could muster up to say.

That year, a little before Christmas, I heard her headed for my desk. The peck, peck, peck of high heels was replaced by the clump, clump, clump of cowboy boots. She made herself comfortable in a chair beside my desk. "Harold and I just bought ten acres outside of town and we are starting with building a house. We even have a barn already there."

I leaned back and calculated all of this and said, "Carol, you have finally reached it." She said, "What's that." "The $40,000 I told you about two years ago." She replied, "Jokes on you Mister Smarty Pants. Harold and I never had so much fun in our lives and it was worth every penny of it."

THE WRECK

SOME OF YOU MAY KNOW THAT I'M A RANCH HAND NOW. I might add that I'm really proud of my employment at the D-Spur Ranch here in Gold Canyon, Arizona. I'm not in the cattle division, however, nor the trail ride division for that matter. I'm in the boarded horses division. Most of my work is in removing used hay. Oh! I do a few other things, too. But too few to mention.

The other day Francis who hails from Minnesota and I were slopping down a little coffee and a few cookies for break. We heard some desperate sounds from the stall area as apparently someone was trying to load a horse in a trailer. With all the thumping, booming, banging and cursing, they apparently weren't having too much success.

Milo Quackenbush was trying to load his horse into his trailer. Frances called out, "Y'all need any help?" Milo responded with a "No, got everything under control." Apparently, Milo decided the trailer wasn't positioned right. So he tied Firecracker, his horse, to a hitch rail that was falling apart, and everyone knew not to use it except Milo. He climbed in his truck and gunned it into a rock-throwing turn and stopped in a better spot. Well, this was too much for old Firecracker. He reared back, pulling the hitch rail to pieces. However, he was still firmly attached to the top hitch rail, a ten-inch by twelve-foot telephone pole.

Now everyone was calling out, "There's a big wreck!" Quite a commotion ensued. Francis called out again, "Do you need any help?"

Milo responds "No, I got it under control." Firecracker was now ballistic, backing up dragging the rail, going down the aisle way between the stalls. The top rail was banging on one side, and then the other. When the horse stopped and Milo strode toward him, Firecracker exploded again. Francis called out again, "Do you need any help?" Milo responded with the same, "Nope, got it under control." Francis looked at me and said, "I don't think so," and went to Milo's aid. Francis easily caught up with the panicked horse, and was successful in getting Firecracker untangled and detached from the rail. Francis passed the lead road to Milo, who wordlessly loaded the horse in the trailer. However, Firecracker was really kicking and banging the sides of the trailer. Milo drove out but he returned about ten minutes later, put his horse in a stall, drove off and I've never seen him since.

There is a message in all of this that escapes me so much that I wonder why I wrote about it in the first place. Just another interesting day working at the D-Spur Ranch.

ALAMO CANYON PASSAGE TRAIL

I HAD MADE A RESOLUTION LATE LAST YEAR that I wanted to ride as many new places as I could in the upcoming year. New challenges were needed in that I've ridden everything locally so many times that they had become old hat. Inspiration had also come to me by my good friend Greg Hersberger, who several years ago said he planned to ride every horse location in the state of Indiana and since has done that.

Here in Arizona where I live, there are numerous trails within an hour's drive from my home. The San Tan Regional Park is only 10 minutes from my house, and the 10,400 acre is one of the most beautiful places to explore in the area. On short notice or during the hot summer days this is a natural destination. Right now, however, I need some new experiences.

The Alamo Canyon Passage Trail is near Superior, Arizona just off Highway 60, and is a part of the Arizona Trail system. I had my sights on this ride for some time and now was the time to pull it off. I'd contacted Harriet Georgopapadakos, who I'd been riding with lately, and after a couple of false starts due to illness and some bad weather that included some ice and snow at our destination, finally got this trip together in January. That Tuesday really was cool, almost cold as I dragged my gear down to the barn to saddle up my horse Lefty, knowing the almost always wrong weatherman who reported good weather had missed again. I'll admit that the longer I live in the Southwest the more cool weather makes me pull on more jackets, vests and gloves; seems I'm always cold.

Soon we were on our way on the 40-mile drive to the trailhead and a climb of 2000 feet. The trailhead is off Route 60 going to the town of Superior. There is a very interesting windmill and set of corrals just as you leave the highway and is picture quality. The trailhead had plenty of room for several trailers and is quite nice with vault toilets and a campground host. We were using my stock trailer, so we traveled with our horses saddled, cowboy style. That allowed us to get in the saddle sooner and on our way.

The immediate scenery was extraordinary. Picket Post Mountain rose to the east at an impressive 4375 feet, and the snowcapped Superstition Mountains were to the north. The winds whipped down upon us imposing a chilly departure. The guide book and signs directed us to a south exit from the trailhead. However, if you should ride here there is a hiking trail that allows horses leaving the trailhead to the east and, though this route is a little longer, it avoids a lot of the rocky wash riding. It is very newly built or perhaps rebuilt with a constant long range view of the beautiful purple hued mountains and canyons. We however started out following the signs and guide maps. This part of the trail is a part of the Arizona Trail, which starts on the southern end at the Coronado National Forest, which is just south of Sierra Vista, and ends in the north at Coyote Buttes, which is between Page and Fredonia.

My guide book stated that you "clatter along rocky washes." I like that word "clatter." My horse Lefty and Harriett's horse Gabby are the same age of 23, and are compatible in that they are very calm and travel about the same speed. Slow. Well they didn't clatter along; they fumbled and stumbled through the large slate rocks that sparkled with brilliance in the sunlight from the high content of mica they contained. This rocky wash riding was a far cry from the normal sandy wash experience normally encountered. We traveled so slowly that we were off our normal mileage pace quite a bit, and we were a little unsure of where we were. Feeling that perhaps a turn somewhere had been missed. Nonetheless, the rock formations and views had us calling out "look at this" and "did you see that." I noticed much more prickly pear cactus and far less saguaro than what I'm accustomed to. Seemed like there were a lot more bushes and the palo verde and mesquite trees were pretty dense, perhaps because of the higher elevation we were at which may have been 2000 feet or so.

We missed our first destination and arrived at the second, which was a set of corrals with a dismantled wind mill. From the numerous cow pies we saw I knew this was still cattle country. The roundups that I have ridden on before made me realize rounding up cattle here would be an extreme challenge in such a rugged area. After a brief stop we continued on our way and began to see some of the most interesting cairns marking the way. Most were very artistically created and some were five or six feet high; one even looked like a man standing along the wash.

A group from the Arizona Trail system was working on the trail, and we were routed into the wash again. We did notice an alternate route back, however, that appeared to miss a great deal of the wash riding. A wind mill appeared before long and this marked our turn around point. Harriet had brought along a lunch, so she made herself comfortable on a rock and consumed it with great relish after offering to share it with me. For some reason I almost never pack any food. This has been a bad habit with me, and one that I have resolved to change. We here in Arizona always pack plenty of water. One trick is to carry a one gallon zip lock bag which, with a little practice, you can give your thirsty horse a sip of water, especially on those hot summer days or on one of those long rides that will revive them to some degree.

We were soon on our way back, and I'll admit the weather usually warms by this time of day, but we remained pretty well bundled up with the winds still blowing a chill down on us. Upon arriving at a newly reconstructed trail that we saw earlier, we left the wash and headed up along the base of Picket Post Mountain. The trail lead us all the way back to the trailhead. The views of the Superstition wilderness lay in the distance of 40 miles or so, and occasionally Weavers Needle would pop up. The late afternoon sun played all kinds of tricks with the colors displayed in front of us, with some golds and purples on the mountains and sky constantly changing as the sun began to retire in the west. This was one of the most spectacular rides I've ever made, proving that life is truly an adventure.

ACCIDENT ON THE TRAIL

SAFETY ON THE TRAIL, USING GOOD JUDGMENT when around horses, and what to do in an emergency are all factors I try to use in my riding experiences. Every now and then something slips up, and it usually takes several things to happen when an accident occurs. My "goes anywhere and does anything" horse, Lefty, and I got into a situation the other day that magnifies the stay alert and keep trail safety foremost in your mind. I'd read an article in the January 2007 issue of the Western Horseman Magazine. The author described a trip to Hackberry Springs up in the Superstition Mountains in Arizona that I had heard about and wanted to visit. The trail was described in the article as well maintained and as a "gorgeous ride suitable for beginners."

I also know a lady who operates the Kings Stable in Apache Junction, which is located at the base of the Flatiron part of the Superstition Mountains. She also told me that trail is a good ride that she often rode. I took this all as a good recommendation to ride to Hackberry Springs. I asked Harriet Georgopapadakos to ride along with me, and she agreed as this was a trail she also had heard about and wanted to ride.

Early February we met at Harriet's place in Queen Creek, Arizona. It was a perfect day for riding, not too hot not too cold. The drive up to the trailhead was very pleasant and only took 30 minutes. We stopped at the Kings Stable hoping to pick up a couple of other riders and reconfirm the trail that we were going to take. Didn't get any other riders but got the trail route down pat.

We found a trailhead without going all the way down to the First Water trailhead and unloaded. Shortly after we were in the saddle as we hauled our horses in a stock trailer, cowboy style, saddled. We came across a very friendly National Park Ranger, who also confirmed our route and destination. He then did ask about the condition of our horses and if we were local or not. There are a lot of winter visitors this time of year, so I took this as something that applied to them not us. This was clue number one.

We continued on our way enjoying the sights and sounds of a ride in a very pristine area but it began to look a little rough in places. Clue number two.

After a bit we came upon a couple of hikers and questioned them about the route we were taking. They told us that there were a couple of very rocky places in the trail that crossed some deep ravines, and that "if" we could cross them the cut-off to Hackberry Springs was just ahead. Clue number three.

I think that at this time I felt that people were just unfamiliar with what a horse could do, as we had already crossed some difficult areas. Now we came upon a very deep ravine with large rocks in the downhill side, and Harriet said, "We're not going down that, are we?" I elected to go first and see what I could make of this. There were plenty of horse tracks and droppings to indicate that others had gone before us. I got to the bottom and Harriet followed and called out, "I don't see a good place to go up." Clue number four.

Lefty and I searched for a way up and attempted to follow where we thought the trail users went most of the time. Stepping up about a foot we came on a ledge about five-feet by five-feet. There was a another rock ledge about a foot up and not as long or wide, followed by a solid rock chute going up about six feet. Lefty struggled up onto the ledge and started to scramble with his front feet in that chute. My head began to pound when I realized he was going down in spite of his efforts. He dropped with his front part of his body in the chute, and his hindquarters about two feet lower than his front. I was off in a flash and didn't step down but actually climbed up and out of the very narrow chute. He struggled to get up but absolutely couldn't get up.

I'll admit my legs were pretty watery as I realized we had a major problem. Positive item number one I wasn't alone. Harriet left her horse Gabby in the bottom of the ravine and began to pull some rocks out from under Lefty. She also had me put a halter on Lefty that she had with her. We then tried to get him up again with no avail. Some hikers came along about this time and one lady took charge of Gabby. Harriet suggested for me to unsaddle Lefty which I did, and this was no small task given the horse was down on his belly and the extremely rough terrain we were in.

Positive item number two was we had a halter, and I was getting help from someone who was a lot calmer than I was. Two more hikers came along and several of us rocked Lefty back and forth, and he slid down the hill to where he could get his feet under him, and he was able to get up.

Positive item number three was both our horses are very calm and easy to handle in a difficult situation. Gabby was now over on the return side of the ravine, and I led Lefty there. All the hikers had gathered up all my tack and carried it down the ravine and up the other side, which I greatly appreciated and couldn't thank them enough.

I saddled Lefty who was not scratched up too much, and I was very thankful there wasn't any bleeding. We were about two hours out from the trailhead, and the way we had come was the only way back. We took it easy and I did get off a couple of times, and led Lefty through some large rocky areas that involved hills.

Once home I doctored the cuts with "stuff," and talked with Kristen Guerra who is an acupressure and chiropractic-trained person. She came out and gave Lefty a couple of treatments, which he greatly improved with. Today he is riding normally, none the worse for the experience.

Harriet has since hiked the trail with daughters and grandchildren, and found the trail got much worse. Well, so much for articles written by people who perhaps never rode the trail, much less a horse.

Remember, life is an adventure, and this is one I could have skipped.

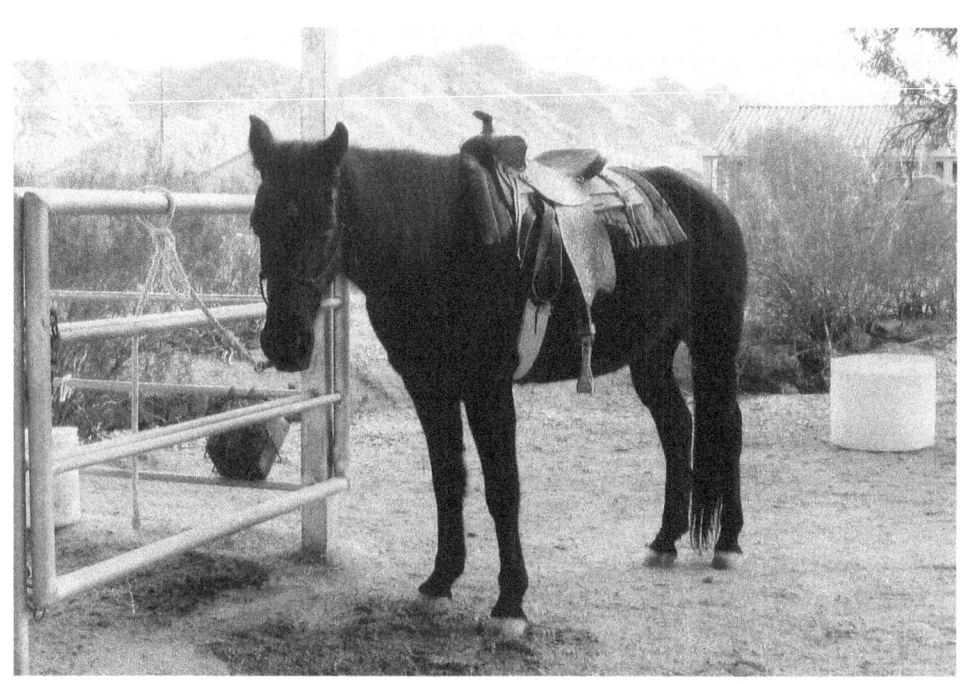
The gift horse Missy. Queen Creek, Arizona.

NEVER LOOK A GIFT HORSE IN THE MOUTH

THE NIGHT WASN'T ONE OF THOSE BRIGHT STAR FILLED EVENINGS that are so common here in Queen Creek, Arizona. Cloud cover made the night dark, and as I was walking around the back of our house, I saw a shadowy figure working around my neighbor's barn.

I called out, "Hey John, how are things going?" A female voice responded, "Is that you Ron?" I realized that this was my neighbor's wife Donna responding. She came over to the fence that divided our properties. I asked her what was new or exciting, and she replied that they were going to move out that Saturday. I told her that I didn't even know that their property was up for sale. Donna then told me that they had sold it out to someone they knew, and the new owners were going to move in late that Saturday. I knew that John, her husband, was out of work and that they probably had a need to sell.

I asked her what they were going to do about their two horses, and that I could they take them to where they were moving to. She told me that was their biggest dilemma at this time. They had listed them in the paper and at the local feed and tack stores, with no positive response. I told her that this was no problem, and that they could bring Missy and Bud over to my place. I asked her to just pay for the actual feed cost, and I'd take care of them as long as they needed. I had a four-stall barn and only one horse, so this was not much of a deal for me to take care of their two. Donna did say that this would be a great relief to her husband, and she would talk to him right away.

I went to bed that night not giving our conversation much thought, except two neighbors that I had enjoyed riding with a couple of times were now going to move away. The doorbell rang early the next morning almost before I had gotten out of bed. John and Donna were there and were expressing with great relief that my offer was a great solution to their problem. John said he was hoping to sell Bud as soon as possible, as this would give him a little cash flow. I told him that as this was the start of summer and with high heat horses didn't sell well at all during this time, but we would do the best we could. He appreciated that and said that he would just give me Missy because this was such a relief to his problem.

Missy was a black 16-year-old walking horse, and when I went over with my trailer I was surprised to see how thin she was. I did know that she was very gentle and easy to work with, and I was really expecting to sell her along with Bud. Both horses loaded with total ease and were soon in their stalls at our place. John now told me that Bud, who was a nine-year spotted walking horse gelding, was kind of hard to catch. I had noticed that when we were at his place, and even with Bud in a stall he had considerable trouble catching Bud and getting a halter on him.

Well, by golly I soon found out he was a pistol to catch and impossible when he was out in the big corral. I kept him in a stall and made it a point to walk up to him four times a day, and catching him several times each time I went down to the barn. As soon as he realized I didn't pose any threat to him, he was easily approached any time I was around, and I could halter him without him moving away from me. I turned him out into the big corral with a halter on, and did about the same thing only this time I fed him his hay. I would let him start eating and would approach him making no attempt to catch him. At first he ran away then moved away and finally let me reach out and pet him. Before long I could hold onto the halter and usually just let it go, so he did not get the feeling that I was there to catch him every time. After working with him on this issue, he was okay in about a month.

The temperatures were running about 110 degrees during the day, and I never rode either horse but kept my contacts up looking for a buyer. Soon after putting the word out on these horses, a lady came along and wanted to try the two out. John had told me that Bud would sort of walk off with you when you got on, so when my prospective buyer started to get on I held Bud by the bridle. He took off running with me hanging on the bridle, and the lady half on half off crashing through the creosote bushes heading for a big wreck. I got hung up in a big creosote bush and parted company with Bud as the lady swung on and proceeded to give Bud an "I'm in charge" ride. I was surprised when she offered to buy him and John took the offer.

They exchanged a check and registration papers, and I delivered Bud to his new home. I told John that I would still try to sell Missy. He said no and proceeded to sign the papers on this 16-year-old Tennessee walker over to me. With a glance at her papers, I realized she had suddenly aged three years in a heartbeat, and became 19. I was not one to look a gift horse in the mouth, and soon found what a great riding horse she has become. Now I've been having some back problems when riding a standard walk/trot horse, but when riding Missy the "gift horse" I do fine. So I've never looked in her mouth either.

A REALLY GREAT EXPERIENCE

SEPTEMBER BROUGHT AN E-MAIL message from Yvette Rollins telling me that Lise Streit may be calling me. Lise was putting on the Arizona Horse Festival and Expo in Buckeye Arizona. Dave Howell, a former ITRA director who is acquainted with Lise, had told her that I was out here and could perhaps lend a hand, but not knowing how to contact me asked Yvette to do it for him.

Well, surprise, Lise did call me shortly after and had some things that she hoped that I could help her with along with some volunteer help. I worked on those things. When she and a couple of her people arrived about four weeks prior to the Expo I drove the 80 miles one way to Empty Acres in Buckeye to meet with her and see what was going on. Phoenix is the fifth largest city in the U.S., and it is a long way from one end of town to the other. Ask Yvette. Lise spent a little time with me and said among other things she would like to have me help Craig Cameron with the Extreme Cowboy race. Talk about something to look forward to; this was an event that my wife Karen and I watch on RFD-TV all the time.

I showed up bright and early November 9th, and was asked to help park cars as they were short of volunteers. This was fine with me because it gave me the opportunity to look for people I knew. The race started at one o'clock, and prior to that all the riders and judges walked the course, and as we did Craig Cameron fine-tuned the challenges.

Since I was the second assistant, whatever Craig told the first assistant he would in turn ask me to do it. With requests like, "Put a cone over there" and "Get a rope for that," I was hotfooting all over the place. I will admit that for all the work I was doing, I was having a ball. The course was to me considerably more challenging than what we see on RFD-TV. My job was to hold up a lariat that was attached to a log for the rider to grab from me and then pull the log to a marker. The rider then dropped the rope and I pulled the log back to the starting point.

After the first ten riders or so I began to drag the log a little slower, and a spectator hollered out for me to get a horse. Believe me, I thought of that but I'd have to get on and off four times for every time a rider pulled the log, and at my age I don't get on and off so good anymore.

I told Craig that I might not be able to do the log pull on Saturday as a couple of loggers from up on the rim had a sick mule, and they wanted me to replace him for a few days pulling timber. Of course, I showed up Saturday and Craig asked what happened to my timber job. I told him that the loggers only wanted to pay me the same as what they were paying the mule, which was the same as I was getting paid for the Extreme Cowboy race. Everybody got a kick out of that.

Sunday brought a new challenge for me. At the end of the course the rider had to load their horse in a trailer. As soon as four feet were in some of them jumped out of the trailer and raced for the finish line leaving the horse loose. My job was to grab the horse and lead it to the finish line where the rider was waiting. Some horses would just stand there huffing and puffing, taking advantage of the break, as they had been running for about six minutes. That meant that I had to squeeze up alongside a big old hyped-up horse that I'd never seen before, and catch him by the reins before he could take off running. Some of them swapped ends real fast and were coming out right behind the rider. So I had to use some of my ITRA type skills and grab him before he could take off. Fortunately, I did not miss a one as they came out of the trailer.

On Tuesday we had the pleasure of hosting Dave Howell and Lise Streit at our home. Dave and I really told some great stories. So, if your ears were burning mid-November, it was because of us. We really had a great visit with them and shared some quality time.

THERE IS A REAL OL' WILD BILL

AT ONE TIME I WROTE A SERIES OF HORSE AND TRAIL RIDING TIPS that appeared from time to time in a newsletter in the Midwest. These appeared under the title of "Ol' Wild Bill Says." Now there really is a real "Old Wild" Bill. I met him many years ago on a small ranch in Colorado.

He was as slender as they come and had to be careful not to slip through the cracks in a floor. His hat was a tangled mess of straw held together by sweat and dirt from being stomped on by various horses and cattle.

Our friendship has lasted for over 57 years. I always called him "Old Wild" Bill because of the fearless way he rode horses and worked cattle. I'll easily admit that over the years I have been envious of Bill, riding horses over the ranges in Kansas and Colorado while I toiled away in big, stinky, smoky, stuffy factories in the Midwest.

So in honor of my friend here are a few thoughts and tips we created together over the years.

OL' WILD BILL *SEZ...*

Pack It In, Pack It Out

IF THAT'S TRUE, how come there is so much trash along the trails and in the campgrounds? I'd like to blame it on some other users group, but

I can't when these areas are occupied and ridden by horsemen pretty much exclusively. Why don't we just place the container or wrapper back in whatever pouch or pocket it came from? After all, it's lighter and smaller now. We need a lot of help on this one folks. So belly up to the bar and pack it in and pack it out.

Get Rid Of That Bailing Twine

WHEN YOU POP A BALE OPEN, pull the twine off and throw it in the trash container. Seems we do pretty well late spring, summer and early fall, but in the cooler weather when we feed more hay, those strings appear to end up everywhere. I don't know how, but they attach themselves to horses and cattle's legs like cockleburs, sometimes getting wrapped up so tight that circulation is cut off to the critters' feet. Other than that tripping them and getting caught in all kinds of limbs and brush. So get rid of that twine before you end up with a problem.

Don't Cross Water With A Tie Down On Your Horse

I SEE IT ALL THE TIME, people crossing water with a tie down on their horse. Maybe it's all right going across a very shallow stream with only a few inches of water, just don't get tempted to go anywhere else in the water. Deep pools and holes can be found almost anywhere, even in the most unsuspecting spots.

I was riding with Ray Deskins, a Northern Arizona rancher on his place in Holbrook. No water anywhere. Believe me, nowhere. We crossed a sandy arroyo only to find it was actually quicksand, and Ray was down to his horse's belly in deep quicksand. If his horse would have had a tie down, he would have sunk into the sand. Ray and his horse got out okay, and I found another place to cross.

Many times I have been riding with people whose horses have stepped off into a deep pool and had to swim out. With a tie down on they would have never made it. Karen and I crossed the Little Miami River in the Cincinnati area many, many times, and Karen always used a tie down on her Arab without a mishap. But we both know now that there are a lot of deep holes in that river, and with a tie down the horse would have never been able to swim out.

Keep Those Barn Aisles Clear

I CAN'T SAY ENOUGH ABOUT THIS ONE. Several years ago I had my horse at a stable that was a newer facility, being only four or five years old. The aisles were totally clear of objects that a horse might accidentally brush against and injure himself. Well, someone got the bright idea that a tack box hanging to his stall would be cool. Then of course everyone else wanted one.

This was followed by hooks for lawn chairs, collapsible saddle racks and then every imaginable gadget that could be purchased from a rich folks' catalog. Now the aisles were filled with boxes, blocks, chairs, buckets, hooks, nails, screws, bolts, boards and metal. Not surprising, horses began to show signs of scratches, minor cuts and scrapes. The picture got worse with bicycles parked everywhere in the aisles, added to which were innumerable golf carts to which, on occasions, I could not get my horse out of the barn from any direction. I was greeted quite often with a "Am I blocking your way" or "Can you squeeze through?" My answer was "No problem." But I eventually took my horse away from that facility.

Keep your aisles always clear.

A Good Horse is Never a Bad Color

ACTUALLY, "OLD WILD" BILL didn't say this but Mark Rashid, a clinician and author, did. "Old Wild" Bill only reinforces that thought. A good number of years I had a sorrel colt born on my place in Tennessee. Yeah, he was a registered Quarter Horse, but not out of spectacular breeding.

He was maybe a little big headed, but straight legged. Still not the best-looking horse I ever saw. It got worse. When he turned two he turned totally black, and I was hoping he would have kept his sorrel coloring. I broke him to ride and found that he had a really great disposition. In time, he turned dapple gray but kept that really great disposition, and was an outstanding horse to ride.

Finally he turned white, and I really don't like white horses. I rode him for 28 years, losing him just after he turned 30. He was the kind of horse that you wanted to be able to ride forever. I really enjoyed those 30 years with him.

Warm Those Bits in the Wintertime

WINTER TIME DOESN'T STOP MOST TRAIL RIDERS. They just bundle up and maybe go on shorter rides. We use the same equipment all year long, including the bit, but in the winter, if not warmed up some, it's like shoving a bunch of ice cubes in your horse's mouth. Not much fun for your horse, and sometimes we wonder why he changed and became harder to bridle. On a 12-degree morning, this may be quite an experience.

I always keep my bridles in the house during the cold months and bring them out at the last minute. When camping out or just going for a day ride, I'll keep the bridles in the truck or some other warm place. If push comes to shove, you can always warm the bit by holding it in your hand, and then you'll appreciate what the horse feels when you shove that cold bit in his mouth.

Campfire Starter

EVER NOTICE THOSE FOLKS CAMPING NEAR YOU? Always seem to have a campfire going in nothing flat, while you can't get anything going despite liberal applications of charcoal fluid and diesel fuel. Here's a helpful hint.

Get a five-gallon bucket and fill it with sawdust, either table sawdust or chainsaw dust. Mix a gallon of kerosene in it and let it soak for about a week. It doesn't hurt to mix it every now and then, as the kerosene tends to run to the bottom. Put a coffee can of this mix under your firewood and a little more in the middle. Light it and you will have a professionally built fire going in no time flat.

Keep Gates Closed or Opened as You Find Them

A NUMBER OF YEARS AGO ON A WINTER'S VISIT to my friend "Wild Bill's" ranch, we set out to do the evening chores. We loaded up his old Dodge pickup with hay for the pastured cattle and horses. Soon we were bouncing along across rangeland covered with patches of snow. The wind was blowing cold and tiny flakes of new snow threatened to cover any bare ground as the twilight crept in.

Upon reaching the first gate guess who had to get out? Since I was the passenger I opened the gate, and with Bill's insistence closed it after he drove through. This went on for several more gates when I realized that there wasn't any livestock in those pastures we were going across. So I said to Bill, "There isn't any stock in those fields, aren't we wasting a lot of time opening and closing all those gates?" He was hunched over the steering wheel trying to soak up as much warmth from the heater that left much to be desired as far as output was concerned. Bill just looked over at me; his face shadowed by the dash lights and replied. "But you don't see me wasting time chasing loose stock either, do you?"

Carry a Camera with You

TAKE PLENTY OF PICTURES; film is cheap compared to the cost of the trip.

I've got more pictures than Carter has pills. There are at least 4,000 in carefully screened slides and another 10,000 in regular photos. The slides are in dated order which makes it much easier to find certain photos. If you do have a large amount of photos you might divide them into three parts: family, horses, and scenic. However, some other arrangement may work better for you. The main point is that ten years from now these pictures will mean so much more to you. Another key item —as told to me by a nationally renowned photographer Darol Dickinson— is that only two or three pictures he ever took out of 100 hundred were worth keeping.

I don't know about the keeping part but can tell you about the missing part. Like the time I ran across a very agitated rattlesnake, or the time I found a Gila monster marching down the trail towards me, and all those wonderful sunsets that I missed because I didn't have a camera with me. You can always throw away what you don't want, but can never recapture what you didn't get a picture of when you had a chance.

Brush Your Horse Every Day

BRUSHING YOUR HORSE EVERY DAY doesn't necessarily mean giving him a show shape brushing. It does however provide an opportunity to check your horse every day for cuts, swellings and other problems that you might overlook when just doing your normal chores around the barn. I just sort of give them a once over lightly and do an inspection at the same time.

In a days' time all kinds of minor injuries can occur, especially if they are out running in a pasture. A horse will also stay warmer in cooler weather with a clean coat rather than a mud-caked coat.

Since we have ol' Dynamite caught up may as well get out the hoof pick and clean the hooves. Here again I don't get real fancy about the job but try to get the frog cleaned up pretty good.

All this can be done in about ten minutes per horse. If you can't do this, call me and I'll show you how.

When Unbridling Your Horse, Unhook That Halter From The Lead Rope

JOHN AND I WERE BURNING UP THE TRAILS one day and when we arrived back at our trailers we got off and began to get the bridles off. My halter is hooked to the lead rope which is tied to the trailer. I simply unhook the halter from the lead rope, slip off the bridle and put on the halter, and then reattach it to the lead rope. John never unhooked the halter from the lead rope that was tied to the trailer.

Well anyway, John's horse Bud took a casual step backwards and the halter was suddenly too far away to get on. John had the bridle reins around Bud's neck but couldn't get Bud to move forward. Now Bud got excited and backed up some more and the bridle reins slipped off. John had to have both arms wrapped around Bud's neck and couldn't afford to let go, as Bud was extremely hard to catch up.

Some nearby folks got his halter and saved the day.

Check Those Trailer Floor Boards

CAN'T TELL YOU HOW DISMAYED AND SURPRISED I was a few years back when I pulled the floor mats out of my wood-floored trailer. One corner was really rotted out, and several other places were pretty soft when I hit them with a hammer. We weren't too far from having a horse have a leg go through the floor. Needless to say, I replaced the flooring before hauling a horse in the trailer again.

I should add that this was not an easy job either. Don't think just because your trailer has a metal floor you are exempt. They can also develop problems with rust, loose screws, broken welds and popped rivets.

Remember if Old Dynamite is willing to get in the trailer, you owe him a safe ride.

Always Carry A Rope And A Halter

WHENEVER YOU ARE OUT RIDING in a non-arena or a controlled setting, it's a good idea to carry a lead rope and a halter. You never know when you might need to tie up your horse for one reason or another.

Not long ago a bunch of us stopped at the Mammoth Steakhouse and Saloon at Goldfield, Arizona. They have hitching rails to tie your horse up, and since I didn't have a halter, I tied my horse up with his reins. I see them do that in the movies all the time. Well, my horse swatted a fly and broke both reins. Lesson learned...

And then there was a time that he took a fall and I really needed a lead rope and a halter badly. Fortunately the rider I was with had one. Sometimes you need to stop and clear a trail. Again, you have that need for a halter and a lead rope. Bring one along with you.

Look Back At Trail Intersections

WHEN TRAIL RIDING IN UNFAMILIAR TERRITORY, always look back when you go through an intersection.

My wife and I were riding at Versailles State Park in Indiana, and we came across a group of riders and exchanged pleasantries. Later we came across them again. This time they admitted they had been lost for about four hours and couldn't find their way back to the parking lot.

The two loops, at that time, were off a one-eight-mile trail that led to the parking lot. They had just kept going past this trail, not recognizing that it took them to the trailhead. So always look back when passing a trail intersection, as it always looks different going out from coming back.

I KNOW HOW THEY MUST HAVE FELT

I WAS RIDING ALONG ON SOME OPEN DESERT land enjoying the tranquility and beauty of the day recently. This was an area I had been riding a lot ever since my favorite destination had been somewhat taken over by hikers and bikers, and had become urbanized. I had never thought of this area as not being remote having started riding there seven years ago, when in reality it was then certainly off the beaten path. The growth in this area however has been totally unbelievable. One Saturday, my "goes anywhere does anything horse" Lefty and I took a ride at the park to evaluate if this was what I thought it was. It was to my dismay to find that it was not. The high vistas that provided great views of desert and farm land were now filled with rooftops, bulldozed roads, and big box buildings. We encountered ten groups of hikers and several bikers all who were very courteous I might say, but completely took away the feeling of being in a remote place.

I needed a new place so I could ride alone to not see other groups of people and experience being by myself. It didn't take any time to find this new place and I began to ride there several times a week. On this fateful day I came across something I couldn't believe. A "BARB WIRE FENCE." It had been built right across the trail and stretched as far as I could see in both directions. Recent hoof prints appeared on both sides of the fence, indicating this fence was really new and certainly not there when I rode here a few days ago.

I know how they must have felt in the 1890s when barbed wire fences sprang up everywhere. They, as I now know, couldn't go where they wanted. The feeling of disappointment, dismay and, yes, some anger filled me as it must have back then.

Joseph F. Glidden took out a patent to manufacture barb wire in November 1874. The severe winter of 1886-87 made ranchers in the West realize the open range days were over, and their stock needed to be "close herded." For the next 20 years fences appeared everywhere leading to the frustration of travelers and herd-driving cowboys. A lot of wire was cut and violence sometimes became a solution.

There I sat wondering what to do. Was there a gate someplace or an alternate route? Same questions folks had asked themselves over a hundred years ago. In my case, the only way back was the way I had come and I didn't like that solution very well. I know how they must have felt back then.

Fence blocking the trail at San Tan Mountains, Queen Creek, Arizona.

I KNOW YOU'VE SEEN THESE FOLKS ON THE TRAIL

YEAH HERE THEY COME, YOU'VE SEEN THEM BEFORE, J.C. "Redneck" and his girlfriend "Pinky Blossom." His small black horse looks like it hasn't been too close to the feed trough in a while, and his coat has missed a few brushings. Not too many cockleburs in his tail however. The saddle looks pretty dried out and the skirts are curled up. J.C. is still riding with his stirrups too short, and it looks like someone finally told him that the bit was in backwards. With one sneaker lace untied and his ball cap on backwards he is ready to ride. The only thing new in the whole outfit is one of those insulated saddle bags that hold up to 12 cans of beer. "Phssst," there goes one now.

Pinky on the other hand is riding an overweight Morgan that is brushed out slick as a whistle. Pinky is striking with line dancing boots, cut off shorts and string bikini top that leaves nothing to the imagination. Her red hat is the kind you buy at a street parade for five bucks. It looks like she is carrying the other 12-pack. "Phssst," there goes one for her. As they passed Pinky asked me, "Want one?" J.C had finished his and threw the can as far as he could into the bushes; "Phssst went another one before the first hit the ground.

We weren't too far behind when Pinky and J.C. took a shortcut off the trail. They continued to short cut at every opportunity and continued to pop a fresh one regularly. J.C. could really throw the old cans a long way off the trail, and I was impressed with his ability.

Needless to say Pinky and J.C. arrived at the trailhead long before we did but were enjoying their liquid refreshments and relaxing. J.C. called out to me that "They need more trails here, not enough mileage." Maintaining control I told him that if they had stayed on the trail they might have ridden three more miles. J.C. told me as, "Phssst," he popped another with a, "Want one?," "Well Pinky and I like a little adventure by going cross country, sliding down steep hills and stuff like that."

I was speechless and could only think about all those empty beer cans that they had thrown off the trail and asked them about that. Pinky said they must biodegrade because after a while they just disappear. J.C. thought that the rain, snow and leaves just covered them up because after a while they disappear. "Phssst," they opened two more with a "Want one?" I suggested that perhaps someone came along and picked them up. They both quickly responded with a, "Nobody would be dumb enough to do that because after a while they will disappear." I responded with, "You're looking at Mr. Dumb Enough." They then noticed my can sticker and two full bags of cans, J.C. and Pinky handed me their empties with a humble, "Want these"?

This article is a composite of actual events. Names and places have been omitted or changed in hopes not to offend anyone. The object is to remind trail riders to carry out any trash that they might accumulate and to stay on marked trails.

GOOD JUDGEMENT IN TRAILER LOADING

SOMETIMES WHEN THINGS AREN'T GOING JUST RIGHT and tempers flare, it might be a good time to call it quits. A few years ago a couple of fellows who I had recently met asked me along for a trail ride. We all kept our horses at the same stable and one of the riders offered to haul all of them in his large gooseneck trailer. My "goes anywhere, does anything horse" Lefty liked to ride backwards in a trailer, so we were going to load him up first. When it became time to load up, I brought Lefty up to the trailer and he absolutely refused to go inside.

I'd been riding this then 20-year old horse for the past 18 years, and had hauled him successfully and easily for thousands of miles. Normal efforts to load him were to no avail. When one of my new found acquaintances began whipping him with a rope, I knew this wasn't right, and I announced I would just take my horse in my own trailer. "Well, let the horse win," sneered one fellow with total contempt for me.

Realistically, I knew that if Lefty didn't load he had a reason not to, and this wasn't a good time to find out why. I didn't want to hold up the others while I gave my horse a lesson loading either. Since Lefty loaded into my trailer with some reluctance, I felt our earlier efforts may have made him a little wary. We hauled the horses about 20 miles and unloaded at the trailhead. A couple of hours later the ride was cut short when one horse threw a shoe. I must admit I was somewhat glad as they were riding rather recklessly.

Ever been in one of these situations? I have, and this kind of event occurred several months later with basically the same group of people. We were ready to go and one horse wouldn't load. Four of these fellows in what I now regard as having questionable experience in loading balky horses began yelling, pushing and shoving. I made an excuse to go home for a minute and to call me on the cell phone if they got ready before I got back.

At home I fixed some coffee, had a light breakfast snack and finished reading the paper. An hour or so later I returned to the barn to find an overheated, sweaty, highly agitated horse with four fellows about in the same condition. The owner reluctantly admitted defeat and suggested that we go on without him. Our ride had been cut short with this loading delay. Sometimes you need to use good judgement about holding up other people just because your horse isn't ready. Six months later the same horse still wouldn't go near a trailer. What about the return trip with a horse acting this way? Don't always count on the notion that he will just hop in the trailer just because you think that he knows he's going home.

Some folks do think ahead some but do not really give themselves enough time and here again good judgement is required. I knew a lady who had a super good looking yearling quarter horse stallion with a nice temperament. She wanted to show this horse the next day. And while he was easy to handle, she had never loaded him into a trailer before.

The night before this big event a friend of mine, "Old Wild" Bill, and our wives went down to this stable where I kept my "goes anywhere, does anything horse" Lefty. She was leading her horse down to her trailer to take him for a short ride to see how he would do. She didn't ask for any help nor was offered any, even though "Old Wild" Bill is a bit of a horse whisperer. We heard the commotion start as we went into the barn to see my horse, Lefty. It must have gone on for 20 minutes or more and then it became very quiet. As we came out of the barn the woman was leading a bruised, cut, bleeding and severely limping horse. The trailer windows were broken out, sides dented and one door didn't look quite right. The horse was ruined for life.

Checking back as to why Lefty wouldn't load into the stock trailer, I found and actually thought at the time that the entrance was too high for him to step in like he's used to. He needed to jump in; simply he just didn't know what to do. One lesson in loading isn't enough. If you feel that you are beginning to lose your temper and trying to force the issue, it's a good time to quit.

And as far as who you ride with, well, riding with people who are careless, well just don't do it. Make an excuse to go back, just tell them those steep rocky slopes or galloping through areas of large stones and rocks isn't your idea of having a good time.

The Stage Stop at Sossaman and Chandler Heights, in Queen Creek, Arizona.

The Stage Coach Route at San Tan Mountains in Queen Creek, Arizona. April 4, 2009.

THE ARIZONA STAGE LINE

RIDING A HORSE IN PIONEER PATHWAYS has always appealed to my sense of imagination and desire to experience the same thoughts and sites of yesteryear. The land in which I now live can be described as being composed of "sun, shadow, sand, adobe and silence." Combine all of these elements and mix in some history and you can come up with some deep thoughts.

Near our first home in Queen Creek, Arizona is the Desert Wells Stage Coach Stop. This stage stop now in crumbled ruins was not an overnight stop or one in which the horses were changed. It was just a place to provide water for the horses and allow passengers a chance to get out, stretch their legs or perhaps take a short nap in the shade of the porch.

The Desert Wells Stop was a plain one room adobe building, surrounded on three sides by a water trough and a porch on the south side. The stage line operated from 1868 to 1916. I am surprised that it ran so long in view of the progress automobiles had made by that time.

The route ran from Florence, Arizona crossing the Gila River and into the shadows of the San Tan Mountains. The stop was then another 25 miles from its final destination in Mesa, Arizona. During this 48-year period of time one can only speculate on the various kinds of people who travelled this route.

I have often picked up this stage coach road while riding my horse Lefty in the San Tan Mountains. And in the shadow of the towering

87

Malpaís, as the late afternoon sun drifted behind the mountains with all of its varied amber hues mixed with gold in the sky, my mind can only wander.

In the deep silence that abounds, I can almost feel the pounding of hoofs, hear the grinding of the wheels and the jingle of the harness announcing the approach of the evening stage. I look for it to round the bend but I can only see where it once ran. Then I wonder who all was here before me? Did this journey change their lives? The untold stories are left untouched.

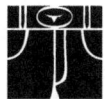

SHEPLERS WESTERN WEAR

A LOT OF PEOPLE DON'T KNOW THIS or even have reason to think about it for that matter. But there was a real live Harry Shepler who had a small western store on the west side of Wichita, Kansas, right on Highway 54. This was back in the days when a person could go into such a place and buy jeans, jackets, boots, cinches, halters, bridles and such at an affordable price.

I was privileged to get to know Harry more being his customer. He had some sort of neurological problem in his neck, so he carried his head somewhat bent, and his speech wasn't too clear. Surgeries hadn't seemed to help much.

I had a friend at that time, AH Bauer, who fancied himself as a bareback bronc rider. There was a rodeo in Emporia, Kansas, and AH wanted me to go there with him in case he got hurt and couldn't drive home; so much for positive thinking.

AH came out of chute number four and the bronc made about four high flying jumps, and AH went skyward looking like a helicopter spinning around. Seems his bare back rigging had disintegrated from hanging in the garage too long. What happened to the "check your equipment" routine?

The next event was calf roping and there was my old friend, Harry Shepler, working as the flagman for calf roping. One contestant came banging out of the gate in record time, swung his loop a couple of times and caught the 400 pound calf.

He swung out of the saddle and scooted along his rope. This is when things fell apart. The horse side passed one way and the calf ran the other way, passing the horse while making full circle around the roper. Then the horse went south and the calf went north. With a bawl the calf said he was done and the well tied roper fell over. Harry waited the required six seconds and dropped the flag.

The calf won third place in roping that day!

DEMISE OF A GOOD HAT AND A PAIR OF BOOTS

Some time ago I noticed the straw was beginning to wear in my favorite cowboy hat. Shortly afterwards, the rim of the crown deteriorated and several holes became evident. As you know, a good hat is vitally important to every good trail rider and cowboy. Needless to say, I was crushed. The hat had come to me via a store in Fort Stockton, Texas. And it certainly was "me," the shape, the straw weave and all. I felt like I had lost my favorite dog, realizing the hat was destined to go soon.

I had a pair of boots in the same boat. These were not necessarily my favorite boots, but I'd had them a long time after getting them at the All American Quarter Horse Congress in Ohio for about $50. When I've got a pair of boots wearing out, and beyond sole and heel replacement, I usually hook on spurs and just use then for riding.

Even the gray boots that I got married to Karen in had followed the same suit. With my favorite hat going and special boots becoming an item of the past, I knew I had to do something out of the ordinary for this passing.

So I shot a hole in the hat and cremated it in a campfire then scattered the ashes around the corral. The boots, well I just buried them in the corner of the corral in a shallow grave.

The replacements arrived but it's just not the same. I don't feel right.

And I certainly don't look right. But with some wear and tear on the hats and boots maybe they will begin to look like me. You know, wear and tear.

Time worn.

103 DEGREES IN GOLDFIELD

WE HAD REALLY HAD GREAT RIDING WEATHER up until a week before our planned over-the-mountain ride. Originally we had set a Wednesday as our date for the ride and found that one of the four riders couldn't make it. The ride was then rescheduled for the following Wednesday.

Not many people ride from Usery Pass to the 1893 Goldfield Ghost Town, located about 30 miles east of Phoenix. It's a pretty rugged ride and ends near the base of the Superstition Mountains. Gary Brown, a native to the area, had wanted to do this for a couple of years. He had found and ridden a part of the route a few weeks earlier. Gary and Al Spall had already decided to make this a one way ride, thereby saving a long return ride, by placing an empty five horse trailer at our Goldfield destination, which we would then use to haul our horses back to the original starting point.

This brilliant plan was only flawed by the rapidly rising temperatures six days prior to the ride. The evenings had been cooling down into the 60s and the highs were hitting the mid-80s by three in the afternoon. Now, the cooling evening lows were in the 70s and hitting the 100-degree mark by noon. This, however, was certainly our last chance to do this ride not wanting to wait until next fall.

May the 21st came up with an early morning cloud cover. I was up at 5:30 a.m. and my wife, Karen, loaded me up with a great, rugged trail

Headed for Goldfield (in Arizona) on a hot day. May 21, 2009.

rider breakfast. She packed my horn bag with one 20-ounce bottle of water frozen. She packed another 20-ounce bottle of water containing just chilled water. Sunscreen was liberally applied to my face and arms. I should have been like everyone else and worn my long-sleeved shirt. My saddlebags contained pliers and a metal comb for pulling cactus from our horses, as they occasionally brushed into them. My camera, a compass and a first aid kit were included.

By 6:00 a.m. I had jumped into my truck and headed for the barn. The temperatures had now risen into the mid-70s. Saddling my "goes anywhere does anything horse," Lefty, I said to myself, "Oh boy! It's going to be a hot one today." I figured the ride should take about four and a half hours, and if we could get on the trail by 8:00 we should still beat the heat of the day.

Al Spall arrived and hooked up his gooseneck stock trailer, and in short order we loaded up our two horses. We pulled out by 6:30 a.m. with me following in my truck. By 7:00 a.m. we were at the Usery Pass trailhead. Al had already talked with Gary on his cell phone. Gary was driving in from North Scottsdale to meet us. He would be arriving at Usery Pass shortly. When Gary arrived, Al and I left our two horses with him, and dropped Al's trailer off at Goldfield. This trip took about 45 minutes.

Back at Usery Pass the fourth member of our group, Mary Hauser, had arrived bringing some great donuts with her. Good way to start a ride. The four of us got underway on schedule at about 8:00 a.m., with a light breeze blowing and with some cloud cover that felt quite pleasant.

The first part of the trail I am quite familiar with. Gary, however, likes to take side trails and wander around a bit. This was fine with me as he was riding lead and would encounter the numerous rattlesnakes in this area first. Strangely enough, on this ride we didn't see a single one.

A few miles down the trail, the views really opened up overseeing rugged mountains, canyons, and even Four Peaks which could be seen in the distance. The wide variety of colors was extremely striking. Along the trail there were giant saguaro, cholla, prickly pear, hedgehog and ocotillo cacti, and mesquite, ironwood, creosote and palo verde trees growing abundantly in this water-starved area.

Some trails get a little rough in some places. May 21, 2009..

After the first hour we dropped into one of the many washes. The deep sandy soil tires a horse easily, and I was happy when we turned south on Jeep Trail 10. The trail is very rocky, and I really don't see how a jeep could navigate such a place without leaving lots of parts behind. Mary and Gary were engaged in heavy conversations as our horses slid down steep slopes and scrambled up the other side. Their conversations remained constant without interruption. I guess that's how it goes with seasoned trail riders in this part of the country.

Two and a half hours into our ride and after a few cross country "let's go over there and look at this" excursions, we decided to stop for a break. Noticeably, there was no shade anywhere. Mary had brought some ham and cheese sandwiches sprinkled with a little salsa and olive oil then wrapped into a flour tortilla type sandwich. Her saddle bags were insulated and she carried bags of ice to keep everything really chilled down. These really hit the spot for a great unexpected lunch.

Gary had us back tracking some, and we ended up in a wash in a deep canyon. We spotted two deer on an impossible-to-climb side of the canyon. There was plenty of vegetation but no footing that I could see. They were about 150 yards from us and had the biggest ears that I have ever seen on a deer. A corner of the western edge of the Superstition Mountains soon appeared, and I guessed we were about an hour from our destination trailhead. Gary and Mary were now into some familiar country, and they were looking for some potholes that contained water a couple of weeks ago. We found them and they were now bone dry. We spotted a coyote about then and he looked pretty dry too. My bottle of ice water was about half gone now, and I really began to feel the heat.

When we topped the hill, I could see Goldfield and we were soon back at the trailer. As we slid from our saddles we discovered that it was now 103 degrees. We all tanked up on water at this point. Saddles were stripped from the horses so they would cool faster. Lefty was covered with crusted and dried sweat. We loaded up all the horses for our trailer ride back to our starting point at Usery Point.

I will admit that we were all pretty elated over this ride which took five hours. It's not a ride many people make, but it is one that we will do again in the fall with a much larger group of riders.

DON'T KNOW WHERE THE TRAILS ARE

WHEN I ASKED HER ABOUT WHERE SHE WAS RIDING her answer was, "I don't know where the trails are."

I hadn't seen this lady for quite a while, but I was sure she was getting some great trail riding in at this one location which I liked so much. Instead, I discovered that she and her husband rarely rode more than a mile from home. "Don't know where the trails are," she said again.

Needless to say, I was somewhat confused by this. Was it that they didn't know where the trailhead was? Simple solution there was to visit the location leisurely by car. Frequently a trail map is also posted along with flyers showing the trails that you can take along with you. Might even walk a short distance on the trail just to get a feel for it.

Perhaps the second part of this person's concern might be knowing where the trails are routed and how to follow them. You can always go just a short distance and turn around and come back. Then do the same thing again, only going a little further the next time. Most trail junctions are marked. So after passing one, look back to see what it looks like if you plan to come back the same way.

Note large trees, boulders, creeks and washes along the way as reference points to indicate you are going the right way, if you should return in the same direction. You might even time yourself to some of these reference points. Should you be making a loop, choose the shorter one first. If you are basically bearing left, continue to do so, even if the trail has cross trails in it.

If your horse is slow gaited, expect to do about three miles an hour. Therefore, a three-mile loop would take about an hour. Walking horses may do five to six miles an hour depending on how much you push them. Of course, the easiest solution to this situation is to find someone who knows the trail and ride with them the first time.

JOURNAL ENTRIES

The Epic Trip to Arizona

HERE AT THE END OF JUNE we are somewhat settled in after returning to Arizona. We had to go to town today and the temperature according to the car thermometer was 118 degrees. It is somewhat cooler up here in Gold Canyon where we now live. It was 111 degrees when we left home.

Let's face it, that's hot. I have ridden in the San Tan Mountains a couple of times now and have enjoyed every moment of it. Yeah, we get up early, ride early and take a long nap before the heat sets in. That's life in Arizona.

Got back home today before Karen, so it's a good time to recap the epic journey when we returned back to Arizona in 2013.

We had really worn ourselves out making all the arrangements, closing on both properties, packing our stuff and saying goodbye to everyone. We also had to make an unexpected trip to Tennessee as my son-in-law died unexpectedly of a massive heart attack. This was just seven days before the movers were to come and pick up our furniture. We were on schedule as our sales contract said we had to vacate the house by June 10th.

Friday, June 7th, 2013

WE WERE READY AS WE COULD BE when the movers showed up at 8:00 a.m. at our Lawrenceburg, Indiana home. Since we had sold or given away most of our furniture and everything else was packed in boxes, we felt they should have us loaded up by noon or 1:00 p.m. Not the case, they didn't finish until 5:30 p.m. or so.

I was about falling down tired and wanted to clean up now that the house was empty. But that didn't happen. We spent the night with our neighbors, Bob and Jean Becker, who had graciously offered to put us up for the night.

Saturday, June 8th, 2013

SLEPT IN LATE THIS MORNING as we were extremely tired from the previous day's moving and packing. We managed to clean up somewhat in the house, but remembering the schedule which now included getting to Phoenix before the moving van. We got all of our stuff in the car and the truck and had a small place in the back seat for Teddy, our dog.

We got to the barn where I kept Lefty at about 10:30 am. Rachel at the barn had fixed Lefty morning and night feed in several zip lock bags. She also gave me a bale of hay. I got the trailer hooked up, hay bags filled and two five-gallon water buckets filled and loaded up. Just as I was about to load up Lefty, Karen said the engine light came on in the car. This was a different light from the maintenance required light, which usually means we were due for an oil change. Something was wrong with the car, just what we needed. We planned on taking four days for the trip. Leaving Saturday and arriving Tuesday as the moving truck was to be here on Wednesday.

Ron, who I had worked with at the barn for the last three years, was a mechanic before he retired and suggested to check the gas cap as it could be loose. Well, sure enough it was. So I screwed it on tight and, of course, the light did not go out. I checked the manual which has more pages in it than the last novel I read. It said after a few trips the light will go out. Darned if after 2,200 miles and numerous subsequent gas fill-ups the light happily still blinked bright on and off.

Being tough and macho and mostly at a loss of what to do, I loaded Lefty in the trailer and that morning we set off. Lefty is a 29-year-old quarter horse mind you, and even though seemingly in perfect health... well, you never know. He stepped right into the trailer, probably thinking this was just another trip to Versailles State Park to go trail riding for a few hours.

We were on the road at around 11:00 that morning. We got up on I-74 and stopped as planned at a previously designated rest stop to check everything. This is something I really believe in doing. When making a long trip, go a short ways, stop and check to see how everything is riding. All was okay. After an hour or so we circled around Indianapolis and picked up I-70 heading west. We made another stop at a rest area and I offered Lefty a drink. He refused and gave me "the look" that suggested he thought we should have gotten to wherever we were going a long time ago.

We now encountered some very heavy rain. The windshield wipers couldn't keep up. Karen following me in our car switched on her headlights and wouldn't you know the right one was burned out. We were in regular communication with our cell phones which were a blessing. I had purposely planned our trip to go through St. Louis on Saturday. Traffic would surely be lighter. We also pre-planned our rest stops and sort of winged it on gas station stops. We paid $4.17 per gallon for gas in Indiana. And our next fill-up in Illinois it was considerably less. At each and every stop I offered Lefty water but he was not interested. In St. Louis we picked up I-255 which by-passes St. Louis to the South and then we picked up I-44.

For several weeks I had called one overnight facility and did not get an answer. Just a happy, chirpy little voice that said "leave a message," which I did and never got a response.

Using my nationwide overnight stabling directory which Jody Weldy gave me years ago, I found another facility just outside Bourbon, Missouri. I called and the lady said she a space and also a fully furnished cabin. Lefty had a grassy hundred foot by hundred foot pen with a shed. I made sure he had plenty of fresh water, filling the buckets in such a way as I could tell how much water he drank.

We had a fully furnished cabin, a kitchen with everything in it you would want. I couldn't find any food, however. Along with the expansive front porch there was a grill. We covered 390 miles that day and so far, so good.

Sunday, June 9, 2013

WE DIDN'T GET OFF TO THE BEST OF STARTS. The bed was very comfortable and coffee on the porch was really relaxing and beautiful. The place was very quiet and relaxing. In fact, I never saw anybody including the owner, who simply said to leave a check on the table when we left. Just horses grazing in the surrounding pastures.

Lefty had eaten well but drank only a small amount of water. If he didn't start drinking more by noontime, I would have to do something. He loaded up like he was going on the return trip home.

We'd been going down I-44 for a couple of hours and here came the wind and the rain. Lots and lots of both. From the one-eyed car behind me Karen said she could barely see me, so I slowed down. Before long the weather cleared and we got to Springfield, Missouri. Joplin would be next and we would pass into Oklahoma. Gas prices had steadily dropped after leaving Indiana and Eastern Illinois. Running from $3.68 to $3.80 per gallon. We had made this trip through Oklahoma many times and something not right always happens. So I had some apprehension and had planned on going through Tulsa and Oklahoma City on Sunday expecting less traffic. Just before getting on the turnpike, Lefty finally took a long drink of water, much to my relief. He was relaxed and ate from his hay bag regularly as I kept it pretty well filled up.

The rest area along the turnpike was closed, so it was a long stretch to Tulsa without stopping. Tulsa has always been difficult to travel as there has always been so much construction, and the roads are identified anywhere from "Will Rogers Turnpike" to "Cherokee Expressway" or to

"Turner Turnpike," and numerous other monikers. What happened to I-44? I don't know. We survived this and made it to the next turnpike to Oklahoma City. Again the one and only rest area was closed. Another hundred mile stretch. The turnpike ended suddenly at Oklahoma City and I knew a rest area was coming up quickly. The traffic was end-of-day Friday night heavy; even though it was Sunday afternoon.

I had to cross five lanes of 75 mile an hour traffic without being able to phone Karen as to what I was doing. I made it, she barely did. I really caught it from her and deserved it. Well, wouldn't you know, the rest area was closed with the gates locked up. We took a well-deserved break at an overpriced gas station.

This part of the country is where you see a lot of one ton pickups with those big ranch guards attached to the front. Saw a number of those pulling trailers with a few bleary eyed cows in tow. Then there are the ranch stock trailers with the canvas coverings on the front half. Horses are loaded with saddles and ropes tied to the saddle. Saw several of these even in downtown Oklahoma City. Outside of Oklahoma City travelling West on I-40 the previous intense truck traffic dropped off to nil. At El Reno we found the tornado damage from the month before unbelievable. Next to nothing was standing along I-40. Piles of junk everywhere and heavy duty billboards just bent over like toothpicks.

Now it got windy coming straight at us. My truck gas mileage dropped to zip. I didn't care as we had gotten through Tulsa, endured the turnpike and passed Oklahoma City without Karen being annihilated in a mishap.

Clinton, Oklahoma was our overnight stop. I had called A.J. Reynolds about a week before and confirmed we were coming and to check directions. I had stayed there before and pretty much knew where it was. The first problem was what was once a country two lane road was now a divided four lane road. I drove through the town without ever realizing it. We were really running late now so I stopped and called. First I called the house, no answer, then the cell phone, still no answer. Waited a minute and called again, leaving messages and turned around and stopped at a convenience store run by a man who barely spoke English and didn't know any A.J. Reynolds or where the main crossroad was.

So we drove around a little and I found a tiny paved road running west. We got on that and after a mile found the place. There in the front yard riding a lawn more was A.J., handlebar mustache, pants tucked in his high topped boots with spurs on. He didn't hear the phone, of course, because of the mower.

Yeah, the town had changed a lot. Some buildings, etc. torn down and the yellow flashing light marking the cross road had been taken down. We were about out of Oklahoma now and my spirits rose considerably.

Monday, June 10th

WE GOT OUR BEST START YET but soon encountered heavy head winds again. The truck skips a beat every now and then and my engine warning light came on. It was really hard to get any speed up due to the wind. We had been going about 70 miles an hour. Gas was down to $3.40. We were now more than half way and I was really enjoying the wide open space scenery. We stopped for the night in a very nice place in Moriarty, New Mexico, thirty miles east of Albuquerque.

Tuesday, June 11th

AGAIN, ANOTHER GOOD START, but not without incident. I was shaving with my electric razor and had the right side of my face slick and clean when the battery died. The left side was pretty shabby and I didn't have the charger or a safety razor with me. So I ended up not looking at people straight in the face, just off to one side or the other.

The landscape with the mountains in the background being a dusty brown, and the spreading pasturelands in front of us also with burnt-up grass contrasting green bushes made you feel like you wanted to saddle up your horse and ride across it.

We had on-and-off heavy winds which is normal for this area. Lefty was eating well, drinking lots of water and had no swelling or trouble with his legs. He seemed to be travelling better than we were. As we crossed into Arizona I should note that no one anywhere ever checked our health papers for the horse, even when we stopped at a weigh station that had a sign "All livestock haulers must stop." We were simply waved through. I figured they will only stop you when you don't have any papers.

We are still on I-40 and Old Route 66 ran through these towns a good number of years ago. I can only wonder what kind of experience travelers from way back had. Now in Arizona the land flattens out a lot. It's deceiving and is a lot harder to cross by horseback than you would think.

Pulling off at Holbrook we gassed up for our jaunt south heading to Phoenix. In reality this part of the trip is devoid of anything. It's good to be on the safe side and be prepared. Unfortunately, the brakes on the trailer gave up the ghost with a loud clanking coming from the right side. Something broke. When I switched off the brake system the clanking stopped. Checking this out it appeared no other damage was done. We only had two hundred more miles to go, most of it in the mountains with some steep grades going downhill. Since we were fairly lightly loaded with one fat old horse, we took Route 377 headed to Heber.

Once I saw a guy riding this rangeland area with two-pack horses in tow. I always wondered who he was and where he was going. At Heber we picked up Route 360 to Payson. Enjoying along the way some of the most spectacular scenery on the trip. Pine covered mountains and deep valleys with those 75 mile vistas.

At Payson is Route 87 to Phoenix. There are some pretty rugged mountains here with long downhill runs and, of course, some long, steep uphill runs which sometimes slowed my old truck to a top speed of 50 miles an hour. Pines began to give way to scrubby to creosote bushes and then finally cactus.

Upon entering the Phoenix area, at University Avenue to be exact, the air conditioning in the truck quit with a clank, howl and scream. This all important item was switched off. I simply rolled the windows down, pulled my straw hat over my forehead, hung my arm out the window and looked as casual as I could, hopefully giving the impression that this was the way I do things. After all, it was only 109 degrees.

Finally, getting to Kristen's place in Queen Creek, where I was to board Lefty for the next six months and unloading we found this was a great relief. Other than being pretty tired, it was a good trip.

Teddy, our dog, was a happy camper all the way.

Our odyssey was over. Our plan on making this a four-day trip, rather than a three-day trip was a good decision. We had two days with heavy rain on and off along with heavy winds. A few mechanical problems but not enough to keep us from finding pleasure in the trip.

ARIZONA GUEST RANCH RIDE

Dark clouds hung low over the Superstition Mountains that morning. The sun was obscured keeping the air cool. It was a good time to take some guests out into the mountains for a couple of hours of trail riding at the D-Spur Ranch in Gold Canyon, Arizona.

Todd, the head wrangler, talks with the guest before getting them on their mounts for the ride. He gives them some pointers on controlling their horses and how to conduct themselves like staying in line, don't cowboy the horse, keeping proper distance between other horses, things like that.

When he rides off to start getting the horses and mounting the riders, I break into my spiel. "Todd will ride up front encountering any coyotes and the poisonous lizard, the Gila monster, and of course he will chase off the trails the numerous rattle snakes in the area."

About this time some of the younger riders get a little wide-eyed and their mouths drop open. Then I report that I will be riding "drag" - last in line in case of an Indian attack as they always attack the last rider in the line. Now the youngsters are *really* wide-eyed and their mouths are completely wide open.

One young boy on the ride looked at his mom and said "Really, Mom?" And she said, "No." I got real serious. Ma'am we've had Indian attacks here before. Now she looked concerned and I continued. The last one occurred 125 years ago. But you never know it could happen again.

Everyone relaxed now and got mounted on their horses. Todd let us out and I scouted for Indians at the rear.

The trail winds its way up into the mountains with many spectacular vistas with views covering the wilderness area of many miles. And you can see far distant mountain peaks. We poked along enjoying ourselves when the rider in front of me said, "Oh, oh, my wrist watch just fell off my arm." I told him not to move. That I'd get it. Nonetheless, he backed up his horse when he pulled excessively back on the reins, cueing the horse to back up. So one hind foot stepped on the watch, and as the horse continued to move, his forefoot stepped on the watch. So I hollered at him to, "Stay still, don't move, don't get off, I'll get it." So he relaxed his reins and leaned forward cueing the horse to move forward. The front foot stepped on the watch and the hind foot stepped on the watch. I was now off my horse and scrambled to pick up what remained of the watch. I handed the pieces to him. He sheepishly said thanks, and I surprised myself by getting my 80-year-old body without a mounting block onto a somewhat taller horse that I am used to from the ground.

ANOTHER ROUND UP IN HOLBROOK

I'M A DYED-IN-THE-WOOL TRAIL RIDER and have been for 40 years or more. But every now and then something comes along that is as much fun and perhaps a little more challenging and exciting.

It was in the early part of December when a fellow I know told me there would be a round up at the Saddle Rock Ranch on the upcoming weekend. That fired my interest up considerably. The ranch is up near Holbrook, Arizona in a high plains desert area. Fact is it is up about 5,200 feet. And to make a long story short, in December it can get pretty cold up there. So I told this fellow I really wanted to go and I'd need to get my ducks in a row.

First thing I did of course was to head home and get the newspaper out and check the weather for the area. I found it was 23 degrees at night and warming to 45 degrees during the day with a brisk wind. There lies the problem. What do you wear? As the day warms, and you need to pull of that heavy, down jacket that felt pretty good when it was 23 degrees, where do you put it? It's way too bulky to tie on the back of a saddle. I was hoping for a warming trend but found the conditions remained about the same as the week progressed.

Here in Queen Creek, Arizona where I lived at the time, the days were getting up into the 60s and 70s, so our horses were pretty short-haired. But along about Wednesday I decided to go anyway. Most of the day-riding crews were going up early Friday morning and that caused a small problem for me. I was scheduled to work Friday morning, and my daughter, Sara, was to be in a school play that night. Checking with my neighbor, Al, who was going up also, he told me he would take my "goes anywhere, does anything horse," Lefty, when he and bunch of other day riders left early that Friday morning.

The plan was now in place for what I knew would be the coldest ride of my life. I went to work that Friday morning almost hoping that the round up would be called off for one reason or another. When I came home from work I checked down at the barn and sure enough, Lefty was gone along with a heavy horse blanket that I had set out for him for that night. Checking the newspapers for conditions seemed to be the next item of business, and they were unchanged. I could see myself the next morning with all that heavy winter stuff and still being cold.

My daughter was really great in the Christmas play that night. And I was glad I had stayed to see her in it. I finally got to bed at 10:30 p.m., and knew it would be a long, cold day that Saturday. The drive to the ranch takes about four hours and I was aware they wanted to start at 7:30 am. My alarm got me up at 3:00 a.m., and I got a pot of coffee going to take with me in a big insulated cup.

I was on the road by 3:20 a.m. The local weather station said it was 60 degrees. Altitude climbing began almost right away from my home and the further up the road I went, the more I had to inch the heater thermostat up. Going up the road on Route 87 to Payson, a person from the Midwest as I am, finds some of the most interesting western names along the way: Mesquite Wash, Camp Creek, Bushnell Tank, Kitty Jo Creek, and Whiskey Springs, just to name a few.

After a bit, I'd made the long climb from 1,200 feet at Queen Creek to 5,200 at Payson. My foot had been on the carburetor most of the time, and the gas gauge had fallen perceptibly calling for a stop in Payson for gas, coffee and fresh donuts. I whipped into an all-night station where I saw the gas was 20 cents a gallon cheaper than in Phoenix. Figure that one out. Getting out of the warm truck, a cold blast of wind inspired me to slip on my down jacket, finding ice on the windshield washing outfit only reminded me of how cold this round up would probably be. As luck would have it, I was too early for fresh donuts and the coffee had been brewing all night, so I just settled for the all-night coffee that could burn a hole in anybody's stomach. I didn't care, however. I was going on a round up, so therefore I must be somewhat of a tough guy. After gassing up and slipping off my jacket and ripping off down the road, ignoring the "Watch for Elk" signs, past Diamond Point Shadows Restaurant, Kohl's Ranch and up to Heber, I swung north at that point on Route 377 for a 36-mile ride to Holbrook.

Dawn came with a gorgeous Arizona sunrise and at 6:30 am I was in Holbrook. The remaining miles took me to a ranch entrance that was a barb-wired gate in the middle of nowhere, totally without note that it was an entrance to anywhere. It was 6:50 a.m. when I swung the gate open, and it was colder than you-know-what.

I'd noticed an awful lot of cattle up close to the ranch entrance at the highway, and I wasn't too happy about that. I knew it was five-and-a-half

Another roundup on the Saddle Rock Ranch. May 12, 2003.

Getting ready to sort cattle, Ron is on the white horse. May 12, 2003.

miles back to the ranch headquarters where the corrals were situated, making it a long ride out to get the cattle. The drive back over a very rough lane to the ranch headquarters finally thumped to an end. Upon arriving I found that the crew had not even had breakfast yet. I was ready for something to eat, and hopefully the weather would warm some. And I felt that this was a good turn in events.

I checked on my horse, Lefty, and then went to the ranch house to join them for breakfast. It wasn't until about 8:30 a.m. when Ray Deskins, the ranch owner, called for us to saddle up. The crew slipped on chaps, strapped on spurs and shortly we were ready. The best thing now was it had warmed up considerably and the heavy, bulky down jacket was no longer needed.

More good news came when the ranch owner told us his brother and nephew had trailered in earlier and were gathering all the cattle that I had seen earlier near the highway, and that they were now pushing them our way.

We set off at a brisk trot and occasionally loped for 45 minutes when we came upon ranch owner Ray's brother and nephew with a sizeable part of the herd. Ray sent the riders in different directions to sweep the pastures clear of any stock.

A young fellow by the name of Jonathan and I were assigned to drive the bulk of what had already gathered towards the ranch. I'll have to say that Jonathan was riding a whole lot more horse than I was. The weather had warmed considerably by this time, and I was feeling pretty good about everything. The ranch is pretty flat but laced with many arroyos and numerous large outcropping of rocks but very few trees. In other words, you can see a long way off.

Jonathan and I were pushing about 75 head toward the corrals picking up a few more cows and calves here and there. The other riders would drive what they had gathered into our main herd bunch.

I'd been having some trouble with a black baldy steer that kept stopping, and I'd have to ride back and get him. He had a big yellow ear tag marked 143. Later on I looked back and there he was standing about a quarter mile back from the herd, which now had about 100 head. Lefty and I rode back and picked him up. This time when Jonathan was going the other way, I got old 143 way over to Jonathan's side and pushed deep into the main herd. About 30 minutes later, most of the other riders had joined us with their gather. I happened to look back and saw that old 143 was standing way back from the herd on my side. So I had to make another long, loping trip back to get him. But before long we got the whole herd into pens and we broke for lunch.

A semi had pulled up to the loading chutes, and a livestock buyer was there looking just exactly like the livestock buyer you've always pictured in your mind. After lunch we separated the stock into five groups. We rode in and cut out about 20 percent of the herd and pushed them into smaller pens.

Now the footwork started. All the jackets and vests had come off now as it had really turned quite pleasant. We ran about 20 head at a time into a pen and then down a chute, where Ray would decide what would be shipped and what would be turned out to pasture. I was helping run stock into the chute. That can be a lot of running around for some of us older folks. Pretty soon my old friend yellow tag 143 came down the chute. Ray called for him to be turned back out to pasture, but when he wasn't looking I sent old 143 down the ship lane. Can't tell you how satisfied I felt.

It sure got dry and dusty working the corrals. But before long we were finished, the semi pulled out with 140 or so yearlings, and we still had a little daylight left. A decision was made to head back home and in a very short time all the gear was loaded up, and after some goodbyes we set off. At the entrance to the ranch I saw one of the most spectacular sunsets I had ever seen, so I stopped and took several pictures.

Al and his crew stopped in Payson for supper, so I joined them. We had a nice chance to recount the day's adventure and what all we had seen and done. Of course, I didn't say anything about old 143. Before long we were back home in Queen Creek after experiencing another adventure in life.

SHELLY AND THE SNAKE

My morning chores were finished here at the D-Spur Ranch, and a lot of times I like to drive to the back of the headquarters area. Just looking at the cattle that might have come up for water, and watching the guest riders string of horses still munching on their morning hay makes for seeing some interesting ranch type activity. It's just a quiet, tranquil time.

As I was just idling along almost to where I would turn my truck around, I saw a snake slithering along crossing my path. Right off, I realized it was a rattlesnake about four-and-a-half feet long. It moved into a clump of cactus and disappeared. Upon my return to go home I passed my boss' home. Shelly was standing out in front and my snake sighting was reported. "Did you kill it?" She asked. I said no. And her disappointment in me was evident. "Show me where you last saw it!" She exclaimed, while she jumped in my truck and a friend of hers, Randi, climbed in the back. While passing the water well, Shelly told Randi to grab a shovel that was leaning against the fence.

Driving back to the clump of cactus, sure enough Mr. Snake was still there. I asked Shelly if she wanted me to drive her back to her house to get a gun. Her reply was that she wasn't going to waste any bullets just to kill a rattlesnake. "Hand me that shovel, Randi," she said. She took a mighty whack at the snake wounding it slightly, but breaking the shovel blade off the handle in the process. The shovel blade landed next to the striking snake's head. Unperturbed, Shelly grabbed the shovel blade and whacked away the snake, ultimately killing it.

She scooped the remains up. I should say Randi and I watched this massacre while standing in a totally safe place, the bed of my pickup truck. Shelly proceeded to get into the passenger seat of my truck with the remains of the snake spilling over the sides of the shovel.

I drew the line here between boss and worker. "Out! Out! Not in my truck with that," I exclaimed. She just looked at me and got out. Then sat on the tailgate of my truck and I drove to the dumpster.

THE TIME I BROKE SOMETHING

It was now fall. Leaves collected wherever the wind decided to pile them. Afternoons brought clear air, sharper colors to the eye, and we wore light jackets to ward off the chill.

I'd been living for a year by myself on a small farm in Western Kentucky. I decided that maybe I needed to do something else to fill my time. In the past, I had some experience green breaking two-year-old horses. That process involved gentling them to be caught, haltered, brushed, having their hooves picked up, sacked out, saddled, worked on a lunge line and ridden 20 times for a total of 20 hours, all in about 30 days.

Two horses came to me from Tennessee and I got started working with them. The gentler one was a black mare of unknown breeding and no name. I started with her and named her Fancy. She was easy to catch, but didn't sack out too well. Picking up her feet was challenge, so I renamed her Flighty. Saddling the mare wasn't too bad but bridling was a chore. Lunge line work was just okay. By now I changed her name to Witch.

One night I stepped into the saddle. No response from her. Pulling on the rein to move her right she exploded, making a tight 180-degree turn, rearing on her hind legs, lunging forward, arching her back and slamming down on her front legs. This was followed by another 180-degree turn and a high-flying buck. This time I didn't come down with her. As I was still flying around in the air, I saw my legs against the blue sky and landed on my right shoulder and neck. Somehow during all of this, my ankle snapped. I couldn't figure out what had happened. While lying there in the manure-filled dirt, I changed her name from Witch to Bitch. Hobbling on my bad left ankle I got her unsaddled and turned her out. Making it to the house and getting my boot off was a priority followed by a shower. By keeping off my foot and resting I was confident I could go to work the next day.

Wishful thinking; I had to call in sick. Then made a trip down to the barn where I had a pair of crutches. Sure made a big difference in getting around. Since it was my left ankle, I had no problem driving and went to the hospital where a young doctor examined my ankle and then x-rayed it. He was very noncommittal, wrapped my ankle and said to stay off of it and come back in five days. He told me almost nothing. So I asked why five days. To get the swelling down so he could get a cast on it, as I had broken a couple of bones in the ankle.

Net result was I had to hire a guy to finish the green breaking and wouldn't you know it. Neither horse ever bucked. So I added two more names to go in front of the Bitch's name.

CLOSING STATEMENT

H OPE YOU'VE ENJOYED THE RIDE THROUGH TIME with me and maybe reflected on some events that stirred your own memories and perhaps some thoughts for new adventures. One thing however, is coming in from a ride and then doing what many of us think about. Having food! So let me suggest these two-time tested recipes you might want to try.

Campfire meal cooking.

RECIPES FOR HUNGRY FOLKS ON THE TRAIL

Ron's Cowboy Beef Stew

(Whoever invented the crock-pot should be given a medal for this one.)

    Two pounds of beef chuck, cubed

    1 Tablespoon of Worcestershire sauce

    1 quarter cup of flour

    1 and half teaspoon salt

    1/2 teaspoon pepper (a little more is okay)

    1 teaspoon of paprika (you can skip this if you don't have any)

    1 and a half cups of beef broth

    4 carrots sliced

    2 onions chopped (more or less depending on size of onion)

    1 rib of celery chopped (more if you like celery)

    3 potatoes diced

Instructions:

When you're ready to start cooking put the meat in the crock-pot first. Then add the flour, salt, pepper and paprika. Stir this up real good then add the rest of the ingredients. Now stir the whole mess up, cook on low 10 to 12 hours for long day riders or on high 4 to 6 hours for the half day riders. Stir before serving.

So basically, you just dump the stuff in and turn it on and then ride off on the trail. When you come back it's ready. Bruce and Jody Weldy will tell you that can't be because Ron only rides for two hours at a time, tops. Well, I like to stir my cowboy stew a lot and I like to get back to do that. My wife Karen, however, always says, "Don't take that lid off and stop stirring that stew." Maybe I shouldn't stir it so much, but let's face it, stirring is half the fun.

Another Good Recipe

I WAS WORKING AROUND THE HOUSE IN QUEEN CREEK, Arizona doing all kinds of important things, like checking the local time and temperature to see if it had gotten over 105 degrees, and counting my socks, stuff like that. I even hollered down to my horse, Lefty, to see if he wanted to go for a ride and got no response whatsoever.

I had the radio turned on to some kind of a talk show with two show hosts talking and laughing all the time about absolutely nothing, when the phone rang. It was Karen asking what I was going to fix for dinner. It was my turn to do so as I wasn't working that day. I fumbled around about that one and said that it was going to be a nice surprise. When I hung up, I realized I would have to come up with something special.

I shut the radio off as it was all I could stand and got the CD player going with some Southwestern Indian music, drums, flutes and such. Then set out to fix some Colorado Chicken and Patsy Potatoes. I'll tell you how to fix the dinner, but you'll have to get your own Indian drum and flute music to set the mood.

Colorado Chicken and Patsy Potatoes

Boneless, skinless chicken breasts (as many as you think your crew will eat)

Wash them off and lay them on a plate

Sprinkle on a little meat tenderizer

Take a fork and punch the chicken breast about 1/2 inch apart on each side.

Place them in a covered bowl adding Italian dressing or Teriyaki marinade sauce to each to marinate them

Marinate them for at least three hours, turning the covered bowl over one time after the first hour and a half. This way they will marinate real good, top and bottom

Then get some baking potatoes (we prefer small ones)

Wash them off and dry them

Spray with olive oil cooking spray

Sprinkle with lots of salt

Get that fork out again and punch them 1/2 inch apart, all the way around

Bake for one to one and a half hours at 400 degrees

Instructions:

Start your coals on the grill. I still like to do it the old fashioned way over an open fire or on a charcoal grill. On the charcoal grill I use 25 briquettes for three to four chicken breasts.

When the briquettes are really gray, I spread the coals out and spread the chicken close to the fire for about five minutes to seal the juices in. Then I raise the grill up four or five inches above the charcoal. I usually cook them for 35 minutes turning them over only once.

If I still have some marinade left, I pour it over the chicken while it's still on the grill after turning. Cole slaw and biscuits are my favorite side dishes. But corn on the cob and a garden salad would fit in real nice too.

The End.

www.ingramcontent.com/pod-product-compliance
Lightning Source LLC
Chambersburg PA
CBHW070031040426
42333CB00040B/1436